Men-at-Arms • 550

The Dutch–Indonesian War 1945–49

Armies of the Indonesian War of Independence

Marc Lohnstein • Illustrated by Adam Hook

Series editors: Martin Windrow & Nick Reynolds

OSPREY PUBLISHING
Bloomsbury Publishing Plc
Kemp House, Chawley Park, Cumnor Hill, Oxford OX2 9PH, UK
29 Earlsfort Terrace, Dublin 2, Ireland
1385 Broadway, 5th Floor, New York, NY 10018, USA
E-mail: info@ospreypublishing.com
www.ospreypublishing.com

OSPREY is a trademark of Osprey Publishing Ltd

First published in Great Britain in 2023

© Osprey Publishing Ltd, 2023

A catalogue record for this book is available from the British Library

ISBN: PB: 9781472854742; eBook: 9781472854711;
ePDF: 9781472854735; XML: 9781472854728

23 24 25 26   10 9 8 7 6 5 4 3 2 1

Editor: Martin Windrow
Map by www.bounford.com
Index by Richard Munro
Typeset by PDQ Digital Media Solutions, Bungay, UK
Printed in India by Replika Press Private Ltd

Osprey Publishing supports the Woodland Trust, the UK's leading woodland
conservation charity.

To find out more about our authors and books, visit
www.ospreypublishing.com. Here you will find extracts, author interviews,
details of forthcoming events, and the option to sign up for our newsletter.

Author's acknowledgements

For his valuable comments on my text I would like to thank Mark Loderichs.
I am also indebted to the Netherlands Institute of Military History (NIMH) for
permission to use data on the strength of Dutch troops.

Editor's note

To avoid visual confusion, *only Indonesian terms in this text are italicized,* but not
Dutch or Japanese.
British rank equivalents are used in the body text, and mostly Dutch and
Indonesian ranks in the captions and plate commentaries.

TITLE PAGE:
Three Indonesian fighters in a machine-gun nest, manning
a 7.7mm Japanese Type 97 aircraft MG modified for ground
use. The gun commander directs the fire using binoculars;
the man in the foreground has a British steel helmet, and is
armed with a 6.5mm Dutch Mannlicher M95 carbine of the
pre-war KNIL. (IPPHOS, 0343)

OPPOSITE:
Kapitein J.H.W. Nix, commanding 1st Tank Sqn at Kuningan,
West Java, on 10 February 1948. The British-style black
beret shows the silver badge of the KNIL Pantsertroepens:
a tank in left profile in a wreath. (Pre-World War II, tanks
had been part of the infantry, but in November 1945
they and the former cavalry formed this new armoured
arm-of-service). His overall is a bleached-out pale OD
Shade 3 American 1943 'special herringbone twill
one-piece suit'. The shoulder-strap slip-on displays his
three silver rank stars placed in a triangle, on the KNIL's
black triangular cloth backing. (National Archives, CC0;
NL-HaNA_2.24.04.03_0_1543-4-4 copy)

Abbreviations (minus those explained at first mention in the text)

AAT	Aan- en Afvoertroepen (transport branch)		RAF	Royal Air Force (British)
ARBAT	Artillerie Bataljon (Marine artillery battalion)		RG	Regiment Grenadiers (KL grenadier regt)
ARVA	Artillerie Verkennings Afdeling (artillery air recon/observation sqn)		RI	Regiment Infanterie (KL infantry regt)
A VA	Afdeling Veldartillerie (KL artillery battalion)		RJ	Regiment Jagers (KL rifle regt)
CGD	Commissie van Goede Diensten (Uniied Nations Good		RPI*	Regiment Prinses Irene (KL Inf Regt 'Princess Irene')
	Offices Commission)		RS*	Regiment Stoottroepen (KL Inf Regt 'Stoottroepen')
C-in-C	commander-in-chief		RVA	Regiment Veldartillerie (KL field artillery regt)
Div	Division		TANKCO	Tankcompagnie Marbrig (KM Marine Bde tank company)
GHQ	general headquarters		VA	Veldartillerie Afdeling (KNIL field arty bn)
Hp VA	Hulp Verbandplaats Afdeling (field ambulance)		VARWA	Verkenning en Artillerie Waarneming Afdeling (ML-KNIL recon
INBAT	Infantry bn, Marine Brigade			& arty obs air sqn)
Inf I (etc)	Infantry bn, KNIL		VERKA	Verkenningsafdeling Marbrig (Marine Brigade recon company)
Infbde Gp	Infantry Brigade Group (Infanteriebrigadegroep, in KL's C Div)		Verk R	Verkenningsregiment (KL recon regt)
KTN	*Komisi Tiga Negara* (Three-State Commission; see CGD)		Vew 2 (etc)	Eskadron Vechtwagens (tank sqn)
Marbrig	Mariniersbrigade (Marine Brigade)		VK-KNIL	Vrouwenkorps KNIL (KNIL Women's Corps)
MARVA	Marine Vrouwen Afdeling (Navy Women's Department)			
4 (etc) Paw	Eskadron Pantserwagens (armoured car squadron)		*Note For origins of these units, see Osprey Elite 245 The Dutch Resistance*	
POW	prisoner of war		*1940–45.*	

THE DUTCH–INDONESIAN WAR 1945–49

INTRODUCTION

Summary

The end of World War II also foreshadowed the end of European colonial empires in south-east Asia, and that in the Netherlands Indies (the vast and ethnically diverse Indonesian archipelago) was one of the first to achieve independence. The new United Nations played an important role in the war of Indonesian decolonization, which was one of the first conflicts to be addressed by the UN Security Council.

In practical terms, Dutch colonial rule had come to an end with the Japanese conquest of the Netherlands Indies on 9 March 1942. During the Japanese occupation part of the European population were interned, and replaced in the administration, judiciary and economy by Indonesians under Japanese control. This process, and a mass mobilization of Indonesians, fed the vision of independence, resulting in the declaration of an independent Indonesian Republic immediately following Japan's capitulation to the Allied powers in August 1945.

The new government of the liberated Netherlands (itself under German occupation from 1940 to 1944/45) was ignorant of developments,

and initially hoped to restore the pre-war *status quo*. However, faced with this unilateral declaration, and suffering from a chronic lack of resources, it was forced to negotiate with the new Republic. While talks at the political level stuttered on, seeking some role for the Netherlands in what was envisaged as a semi-independent Indonesia, the deep-seated political disagreements ensured a parallel and almost continuous armed struggle, despite a nominal ceasefire in 1946–47. Dutch military operational successes, mainly on Java and Sumatra (the most populous and developed islands) failed to break the Republic's determination, and the Netherlands became politically isolated from international support. Faced with a deadlock and under UN pressure, the parties ultimately reached a political agreement, and, after a war lasting more than four years, the Netherlands transferred sovereignty to Indonesia in December 1949.

The conflict was extremely violent on both sides. At least 97,400 Indonesian combatants and civilians lost their lives. On the Dutch side, 2,777 troops were killed and 2,504 died as a result of disease or accident; in total, 5,281 KL and KNIL soldiers lost their lives (excluding in the 1945 *Bersiap* killings – see below, 'The Course of the War'): so perhaps, a Dutch/Indonesian ratio of 1:35. In the words of historian Rémy Limpach, the Dutch made use of 'mass violence... structurally and on a large scale'.

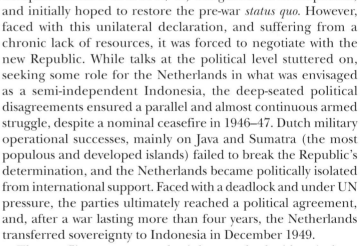

3

CHRONOLOGY

1945:
15 Aug Capitulation of Japan.
17 Aug Proclamation of Republic of Indonesia.
29 Sept British Indian Army troops land in Jakarta to take Japanese surrender.
1 Oct British Gen Christison recognizes the *de facto* Republican administration.
10 Oct British Indian troops land at Medan and Padang.
15–19 Oct First battle of Semarang.
18 Oct British Indian troops arrive in Bandung.
19 Oct British Indian troops land at Semarang.
25 Oct British Indian troops land at Surabaya and Palembang.
28–29 Oct First battle of Surabaya.
31 Oct–2 Nov Battle of Magelang.
10–29 Nov Second battle of Surabaya.
18–21 Nov Second battle of Semarang.

1946:
16–25 July Malino conference.
14 Oct Nominal ceasefire.
15 Nov Draft Linggarjati Agreement (foreseeing Dutch–Indonesian federal structure).
29 Nov Last British Indian troops leave Indonesia.

1947:
21 July–4 Aug Dutch offensive, Operation 'Product'.
1 Aug UN Security Council Resolution 27: call to cease hostilities and settle dispute by arbitrated negotiation.

25 Aug Arbitration committee established by UN Good Offices Commission (CGD).

1948:
17 Jan 'Renville' armistice agreement: recognition of existing demarcation lines, evacuation of Republican troops from West and East Java.
9 Mar Installation by Dutch of Provisional Federal Government.
18–30 Sept Madiun uprising against Republican government.
19 Dec–3 Jan 1949 Dutch offensive, Operation 'Crow'; Yogyakarta taken, Republican leaders captured.

1949:
28 Jan Security Council Resolution 63 adopted: ceasefire; release of Republican leaders; establishment of interim Federal government; elections, then transfer of sovereignty.
1 Mar Republican attack on Yogyakarta.
7 May Van Roijen–Roem statement: cessation of hostilities from 3 August 1949.
11 & 15 Aug Cessation of hostilities on Java & Sumatra officially in force.
23 Aug–2 Nov Round-Table Conference in The Hague.
27 Dec Transfer of sovereignty.
1950:
26 July Royal Netherlands–Indonesian Army (KNIL) disbanded.

REVOLUTION

The Japanese surrender in the absence of Allied troops left a power vacuum lasting several weeks, which allowed the nationalists to begin shaping a Republican government. Two days after the Japanese capitulation, on 17 August 1945, the nationalist leaders Soekarno and Mohammad Hatta proclaimed Indonesian independence in the capital, Batavia (Jakarta). This declaration of independence gave them the political initiative, which they would never relinquish. The next day a constitution was adopted: Indonesia would become a unitary state, with a presidential democracy and a secular character. On 4 September a government was formed with Soekarno as president; this largely secured the support of the Indonesian administrators in place, and of some traditional community leaders.

Meanwhile, during 19–25 August the Japanese ordered the demobilization of their wartime Indonesian auxiliaries: the Kyōdo Bōei Giyûgun ('Volunteer Army for Defence of the Fatherland' – hereafter, for short, the Giyûgun), known in Indonesian as the *Tentara Sukarela Pembela Tanah Air (PETA),* and the weaker Heiho ('auxiliary soldier') units. Although the auxiliaries were tainted in the eyes of some by their closeness to the Japanese, this decision cost the fledgling Republic a chance to take over an existing lightly armed and trained military force. The only Indonesians now officially under arms were the police, which accepted Republican authority during September/October.

On 22 August 1945, the *Badan Keamanan Rakjat (BKR*, 'Organization for the People's Security') was established. In order not to provoke either the Japanese or the Allies, this was not a national army, but a decentralized organization tasked with 'maintaining security with the help of the people and the relevant government bodies'. The central government in Jakarta (later in Yogyakarta) had little influence over the *BKR*, which was answerable to local and regional political structures. The units were formed by ex-officers from the former Giyûgun, Heiho, Seinendan (youth corps) and other Japanese-created bodies. These leaders derived their positions in the hierarchy from the local loyalty they commanded, personal relationships, and the relative firepower available to their units.

From mid-September 1945 the *BKR* and irregular groups armed themselves from Japanese sources. Some weapons were captured, but in October the Japanese garrison in Surabaya simply handed theirs over, and other units in Central Java also provided limited armament to enable nationalists to 'maintain law and order'. Significantly, the arming of the Indonesian revolution was thus not top-down by the government, but bottom-up by local organizations, with the drawbacks which that entailed.

Proklamasi: **the future President Soekarno proclaims the Indonesian Republic's independence in Batavia (Jakarta) on 17 August 1945. On the right, in white, is his deputy Mohammad Hatta. In the uncropped photo, a captain of the Giyûgun battalion in Jakarta is seen at far left. (NIMH, 2164-003-008)**

FOREIGN FORCES, 1945–46

JAPANESE ARMY OF OCCUPATION

When Japan capitulated, the Imperial Japanese Army's Sixteenth Army occupied Java, the Twenty-Fifth Army was on Sumatra, and the Imperial Japanese Navy's Second Southern Expeditionary Fleet was responsible for the other islands. At the end of October 1945, IJA strength throughout the archipelago was nearly 290,700 men (including civilian employees), of whom 73,000 were on Java and nearly 70,000 on Sumatra; at its Surabaya base the IJN had 3,110 military and 1,455 civilian personnel. The IJA had divided Java territorially, into Jakarta District and three Sectors.

Police and auxiliary forces

After October 1942 the Japanese had amalgamated the various colonial police forces into one, officered by Japanese who were often transferred from Formosa (Taiwan). The police on Java counted 26,998 men; among them, each local administrative command ('residence') had a company, 60 to 150 strong, of the heavily armed mobile police (Tokubetsu Keisatsutai, 'Special Police Force'), with Indonesian rank-and-file and

Revolutionary *pemudas* and *pemudis,* late 1945, wearing civilian clothing and armed with pre-war KNIL 6.5mm M95 carbines. The man at far right carries a Japanese military sword, possibly one of those made in Indonesia during the occupation. (IPPHOS, 0064)

Japanese officers. Among the Japanese-formed local auxiliary services, the Heiho on Java had 24,873 men. The Giyûgun had 66 autonomous territorial infantry battalions on Java and Madura and three on Bali, totalling 37,479 men, with company-size units on Sumatra.

After capitulation

After previously allowing Indonesians only an advisory role in government, on 7 September 1944 Tokyo had promised the East Indies independence, but no practical progress was made until shortly before the end of the war. After its capitulation the IJA ruled out further support for the Indonesian quest for independence. (Nevertheless, Rear Adm Maeda Tadashi, the IJN commander in West Java, advised Soekarno and Hatta on the eve of their independence proclamation, and effectively took them under IJN protection.)

Sixteenth Army would partially self-intern, concentrating most of its troops outside the major cities, and partly disarming them on 29 August to avoid clashes with Allied troops when they arrived. Small armed units would remain in the cities to maintain order alongside the Indonesian police. In light of the increasing violence, however, this limit on their responsibility was revoked on 18 September.

The arrival of the first British Indian Army troops on 29 September drastically changed the political and military situation. The Sixteenth Army expected to be disarmed and repatriated, but instead remained responsible for maintaining public safety. In the event, the British were forced by shortage of manpower to deploy Japanese troops in arms, not only for static security tasks but also offensively, even including some use of artillery and armour. Without Indonesian support it was still impossible for the Japanese to maintain public order, and they advised the British to involve the Indonesians in this task and to recognize their desire for independence. Lieutenant-General Sir Philip Christison, commanding the British troops in the Netherlands Indies, announced on 1 October that 'The Indonesian Government would not be expelled, and would in fact be expected to continue the civil administration in those areas not occupied by British forces.' Sixteenth Army HQ interpreted this *de facto* British recognition on 3 October by issuing Army Order No. 1149: that the Indonesians should maintain public safety with limited assistance from IJA troops, who could lend them weapons. ('Lending' weapons presupposes the ability to get them back, but this would turn out to be wishful thinking.)

In East Java, the nationalists took over Surabaya on 1–2 October 1945; the East Java Sector Force and part of the Second Southern Expeditionary Fleet – approximately 14,000 Japanese personnel, with their weapons – fell into Indonesian hands. In Central Java, the Sector Force commander at Magelang was forced to surrender on 13 October. The commander at Semarang, Maj Kido Shinichirō, refused to hand over his weapons; on 15 October he took the offensive, and regained control of the city after five days' fighting. No large-scale transfer of weapons took place in West Java, where, on 10 October, the Sector Force restored public order, controlling Bandung until the arrival of British troops.

The arriving Allies did not give the Japanese the legal status of POWs, but of 'Japanese surrendered personnel' (JSP). This 'saved face', but it deprived the JSP of their legal protection under the Geneva Convention and the Potsdam Declaration. This JSP status gave the Allies license to deploy Japanese soldiers for their own military and/or economic purposes. During April–July 1946, Allied Forces Netherlands Indies evacuated the JSP, and 30,000 Japanese prisoners in Indonesian hands, from the ports of Jakarta, Surabaya and Semarang to Japan, Korea and Formosa. Exceptions were JSP who had been handed over to the Dutch as workers (still numbering 13,678 on 1 January 1947), and 3,059 detained as suspected war criminals.

Between the Japanese capitulation and repatriation, just over 1,100 IJA and IJN personnel and civilian employees were killed, committed suicide, or died from illness or accidents. (This total was roughly twice the 596 suffered during their conquest of the Netherlands Indies in 1942.)

This British officer is identified as a Capt Tomlinson, photographed with (right) Maj Kido Shinichirō, Japanese commander at Semarang, Central Java, after the second battle there on 18–21 November 1945. During the first battle (15–19 October), Kido had brought the city back under Japanese control in fierce fighting with Indonesian nationalists. (NIMH, 2158_101841)

BRITISH INDIAN ARMY

At the Potsdam Conference in July 1945 the Allies handed responsibility for the Japanese-occupied southern countries to South-East Asia Command, under the British Adm Lord Louis Mountbatten, with effect from 15 August. The British had not anticipated any power vacuum after their expected military conquest, but the A-bombs and the early Japanese capitulation caught them unprepared, and SEAC faced serious shortages of manpower and shipping. There was no question of their immediate occupation in strength of British Malaya and Borneo, Siam (modern Thailand), southern Indochina and the Netherlands Indies.

SEAC's missions in Indonesia were to accept the local Japanese surrender; disarm and repatriate Japanese troops; liberate and repatriate Allied POWs and civilian internees; and transfer administration to the Netherlands Indies government. The Australian I Corps (7th & 9th Divs) in Borneo was assigned the eastern islands, including Sulawesi (Celebes). The British XV Indian Corps would occupy Sumatra, Java, Madura, Bali and Lombok; a division each were assigned to Sumatra and Java, but these would only become available after the priority re-occupation of Malaya. Before their arrival, RAPWI parties (Recovery of Allied Prisoners of War & Internees) were parachuted in on Sumatra and Java. These

A column from 23rd Indian Inf Div, led by an M3A3 light tank, near Bekasi east of Jakarta on 29 November 1945. Six days previously an RAF C-47 'Dakota' had made an emergency landing nearby, and the *Banteng Hitam* ('Black Buffalo') armed group had killed 20 surviving Indian infantrymen of the 2/19th Kumaon Bn and five aircrew. The resulting searches over several days were carried out in a vengeful spirit, with villages burned down. (IWM CF 1277)

were mixed British–Dutch teams, tasked with locating the camps and preparing their evacuation. However, evacuation of Dutch prisoners and internees from Indonesia was not foreseen, since the Allies assumed the re-establishment of Dutch authority.

It was not until the end of September 1945 that it became clear to SEAC that the declaration of the independent Indonesian Republic had created an entirely new reality on the ground. On 28 September Adm Mountbatten revised the orders for XV Indian Corps: they would not attempt to occupy all of Java and Sumatra, but would limit themselves to urban enclaves essential to the execution of their core missions. Outside these key areas, no troops would be deployed to restore Dutch sovereignty. Eventually the cities of Jakarta (Batavia), Bandung, Semarang and Surabaya on Java were occupied, and Medan, Padang and Palembang on Sumatra.

In October 1945, XV Indian Corps was renamed Allied Forces Netherlands East Indies (AFNEI), commanded by Gen Christison. The Burma veterans of 23rd & 26th Indian Inf Divs were assigned to Java and Sumatra respectively; they would be reinforced by 5th Indian Inf Div, 5th Indian Para Bde and 50th Indian Tank Bde, while 80th Indian Inf Bde would relieve the Australians at Makassar in South Sulawesi in February 1946. The combat strength of AFNEI was about 45,000 men.

The first troops arrived in Jakarta on 29 September, and on 1 October Gen Christison's announcement (above) gave *de facto* recognition to the Republican regime. Key cities were occupied, and in order to evacuate POWs, internees and surrendered Japanese the British moved further inland from Jakarta and Semarang. However, the British Indian troops soon found themselves caught in the middle of a nationalist revolution, and were attacked in strength by armed Indonesian groups. Faced with fierce opposition, some British Indian troops resorted to drastic measures. According to British historian Richard MacMillan: 'Throughout the occupation, burning of villages… and executions of prisoners became a matter of routine.'

Anticipating extreme Indonesian reactions to the arrival of fresh Dutch troops, on 9 November Gen Christison temporarily banned Dutch landings in Java and Sumatra, and the first slowly-arriving elements of the Netherlands Royal Army were diverted to Malaya. It was not until 9 March 1946 that the takeover of the British enclaves by Dutch troops began on Java, and the last British Indian soldiers did not leave until 29 November 1946. British and Indian casualties amounted to 2,353 men, of whom 620 were killed, 1,331 wounded and 402 missing. In addition, 746 Indian soldiers deserted. The Indian nationalist leader Jawaharlal Nehru, whose own political campaign for Indian independence would succeed on 15 August 1947, had expressly objected to the involvement of Indian troops.

DUTCH RECOLONIZATION

Political strategy

After the proclamation of the Indonesian Republic, it was clear to progressive Dutch politicians that the political relationship with Indonesia would have to change radically, and this was initially considered as part of a potential constitutional reform including the Netherlands itself. They envisaged a new 'commonwealth' or Dutch–Indonesian union, comprising the four parts of the Netherlands and the colonies in the Netherlands Indies and Suriname and Curacao (Netherlands Antilles), with the constituent parts enjoying a degree of autonomy over internal affairs. In the event, this ambitious vision was not realized, but hopes of implementing the Indonesian aspect formed the background to events throughout the conflict.

At the suggestion of their lieutenant governor-general in Indonesia, Dr Hubertus van Mook, the Dutch government decided on 10 February 1946 to reorganize Indonesia itself as a federation of semi-autonomous states, with a representative of the Dutch Crown as head of government. This federal structure would last for a limited period of time, its duration to be a matter of mutual agreement. Van Mook's federal policy received support at the Malino conference (July 1946) from representatives of Dutch Borneo and East Indonesia, and subsequently formed the basis for the draft Linggarjati Agreement between the Netherlands and the Republic of Indonesia on 15 November 1946. The Republican representatives agreed that a federal United States of Indonesia might become a component of a Dutch–Indonesian Union. However, long before this outline could be fleshed out, fatal disagreements soon arose. The Dutch parliament imposed additional conditions, which Indonesia rejected. The Republic, in turn, rejected the proposals for its limited sovereignty over foreign relations and its armed forces. While discussions continued between the various interested parties, and some 'outer' federal states *(negara)* were instituted, fighting continued.

Dr H.J. van Mook, born at Semarang in 1894, joined the Netherlands Indies administrative service in 1918 and rose to a senior post, but left Java before the defeat in 1942. In the forefront of reformist Dutch civil servants, with deep local knowledge and a tireless work ethic, he served as lieutenant governor-general from 1945 to 1948. Van Mook was the driving force behind negotiations with moderate Indonesians, and attempted to safeguard Dutch involvement in a future independent Indonesia. (National Archives, Anefo Photo Collection)

Civil administration

Alongside the British, the NICA (Netherlands Indies Civil Administration) also arrived on Java and Sumatra, with the task of administering reoccupied territory. Until 1942 colonial government had been based on cooperation between Dutch officials and traditional feudal community chiefs, but restoring it proved impossible. The perceived legitimacy of Dutch colonial authority had been virtually destroyed by the crushing Japanese victory in 1942, and by the nationalist mobilization of Indonesians during the Japanese occupation. In practice, an alternative independent Indonesian administrative apparatus and armed forces had functioned on Java and Sumatra since the Japanese capitulation, and the proclamation of the Republic was widely welcomed (though variously interpreted) across the archipelago.

In addition to its weakened popular authority, on the practical level the restoration of a Dutch-led civil service was greatly hindered by a shortage of Dutch personnel. Deaths during the occupation, followed by retirements, had roughly halved their numbers (e.g., to only 105 on Java and Madura in November 1948), and new recruits were insufficient to replace them. Additionally, in Aceh (North Sumatra) and on that island's east coast, a social revolution took place in 1945, which saw many traditional leaders murdered. The involvement of Indonesian officials in the administration was Dutch policy, but few were willing to cooperate, since this put them in grave danger of kidnapping or assassination by nationalists. These obstacles, and a general lack of resources, prevented any significant Dutch penetration into Indonesian society, or the rebuilding of an efficient administration.

Police

By 1 January 1947 the pre-war colonial police strength had sunk to 10,951. Small local units were formed in the 'Outer Regions' after the Japanese surrender, and after the British withdrawal from Java and Sumatra recruitment began in each 'residence'. For the reoccupation of territory after Operation 'Product' in mid-1947, 110 mobile police squads were assembled from the existing force, and formed the cores of new territorial units. The same happened following the further reoccupation of Republican territory in Op 'Crow' in 1948/49. Although police strength had roughly tripled by that date, it was still an understrength force spread over an ever larger area.

As the Dutch military and the police proved incapable of suppressing the increasing insecurity in the countryside, Dutch agricultural companies set up 'estate guards' (Ondernemingswachten), but from January 1948 the government took over their organization. These armed groups of private employees ranged in strength from 10 to 30 men per estate; in 1949 there were 859 estate guard units on Java and Sumatra, with a combined strength of 22,443. The Dutch military wanted to transfer its static surveillance tasks to the police and estate guards, but neither of these paramilitary organizations had sufficient training, leadership or armament for such duties.

INDONESIAN FORCES

Successive reorganizations

The Republican government had little control over local developments throughout its huge territories, and lacked a properly functioning central military organization. In several rounds of reforms (see panel) it attempted to build a centrally-controlled military apparatus, with varying results.

The first *Tentara Keamanan Rakjat* (*TKR*, 'Army for the People's Security') was established on 5 October 1945. This introduced a national army, with (on paper) a hierarchical command structure controlled centrally from a Ministry of Public Security and the *Markas Tertinggi* (Supreme Headquarters). Java, the cockpit of the revolution, was divided into three territorial commands totalling ten divisions, and Sumatra was a territorial command with six divisions. In practice,

Designations of Indonesian Republican forces

Abbr.	Name, Indonesian	Name, English	Date
BKR	*Badan Keamanan Rakjat*	Organization for the People's Security	22 August 1945
TKR	*Tentara Keamanan Rakjat*	Army for the People's Security	5 October 1945
TKR	*Tentara Keselamatan Rakjat*	People's Security Army	7 January 1946
TRI	*Tentara Republik Indonesia*	Army of the Republic of Indonesia	26 January 1946
TNI	*Tentara Nasional Indonesia*	Indonesian National Army	5 May 1947
APRIS	*Angkatan Perang Indonesia Serikat*	Armed Forces of the Federal Republic of Indonesia	27 December 1949

however, this organization failed in the bud. The authority of the three territorial commanders on Java was not recognized by local subordinates; centrally-appointed divisional commanders were often rejected, and the operational development of the nominal divisions never got off the ground. The army commander himself was a beneficiary of this insubordination: on 12 November 1945 an ex-Giyûgun battalion commander, Raden Sudirman, was elected *TKR* supreme commander (*panglima besar*) by regional officers, his election only reluctantly being ratified by the central government on 18 December.

On 26 January 1946 the national army was reorganized as the *Tentara Republik Indonesia* (*TRI*, 'Army of the Republic of Indonesia'). The Ministry of Public Security became the Ministry of Defence and of the Armed Forces. In fact, two competing chains of command emerged: that of Amir Syarifuddin as defence minister, and that of Gen Sudirman's *Markas Besar Tentara* (Army Headquarters). The reorganization involved reducing the number of divisions on Java to seven, and on Sumatra to three. The military police were placed directly under Ministry control.

The arrival of Syarifuddin as defence minister began a long conflict between the political leadership and the military. He stood for an army imbued with democratic socialist ideals, enjoying – as an embodiment of the popular will for freedom – a special role in the revolution, but loyal to the government. However, Gen Sudirman did not see himself in any way as a subordinate to the political leadership, but as at least their equal. Also, in opposition to the government, Sudirman rejected the strategy of negotiations with the Dutch.

On 5 May 1947 the *TRI* was again redesignated, as the *Tentara Nasional Indonesia* (*TNI*, 'Indonesian National Army'). This plan envisaged the

The Republican *Pucuk Pimpinan TNI* (Armed Forces Council) after its installation on 28 June 1947. (Left to right:) Air Cdre Raden Suryadi Suryadarma, Air Force chief of staff; LtGen Urip Sumoharjo, chief of general staff; MajGen Sutomo; Gen Sudirman, commander-in-chief; MajGen Sakirman, head of *TNI Masyarakat* ('People's Armed Forces'); R Adm Mohammad Nazir, Navy chief of staff ; MajGen Djoko Suyono, head of *Biro Perjuangan* ('Bureau of Struggle'), Ministry of Defence. Generals Sutomo, Sakirman and Djoko Suyono represented the *laskar* element in the nationalist forces. (NIMH, 2155_800272)

Kolonel Abdul Haris Nasution, a member of the Batak ethnic minority in North Sumatra. He studied at the KNIL officers' academy (KMA) in Bandung, and joined the Republican army in 1945, taking command of the *Siliwangi* Div in 1946. Appointed deputy commander of Mobile Forces in 1948, he would play a leading part in formulating the intended *TNI* reorganization programme, and in its guerrilla strategy. Due to Gen Sudirman's incapacity through illness, Nasution was thereafter effectively in command of the Republican military. (IPPHOS, 0314)

amalgamation into the *TNI* of the non-state armed groups (see below) to form a single national military organization, under the collective leadership of the *Pucuk Pimpinan TNI* ('Armed Forces Council'). Chaired by Gen Sudirman, this consisted of representatives of the Ministry and the three armed forces, and three representatives of the *laskar* armed groups, including Gen Sumitomo ('Bung Tomo'), former leader of the *PBRI* in the battles of Surabaya. Two months later, Operation 'Product' seriously changed the situation on the ground in the Netherlands' favour.

Under the subsequent Renville Agreement, *TNI* troops would be evacuated from West and East Java into a reduced Central Java (inadequate to feed, clothe and house them). On 2 January 1948 the Republican government announced a *Rekonstruksi dan Rasionalisasi (RERA)* programme. The *RERA* aimed to strengthen the Ministry of Defence in relation to Gen Sudirman, and also to increase the army's effectiveness by reducing its numbers in order to concentrate its available weapons and resources. The leadership was to be reorganized into the *Angkatan Perang Staff* ('Armed Forces Staff'), controlling the chiefs-of-staff and the territorial forces directly under the Ministry of Defence; and the Operational Command *(Komando Operatif)* under Gen Sudirman. However, Sudirman's supporters were able to enforce his domination over the army; the rest of the *Angkatan Perang Staff* became entirely subordinate to him, and the partial demobilization plan was dropped.

Given the new balance of territory, doctrinal planning was then revised by a group of formerly KNIL-trained officers under Sudirman's able new deputy, Col Abdul Haris Nasution, and his close comrade Col Tahi Bonar Simatupang. Colonel Nasution envisaged a change from conventional warfare supplemented by guerrilla activity, into a guerrilla war in three classic 'Maoist' phases. The first would be defensive, concentrating on survival and the securing of logistics. In the second, guerrillas would consolidate into larger units, seeking opportunities to attack Dutch convoys and posts piecemeal and capture their equipment. Once this phase had accomplished a deadlock, a third offensive phase would see the guerrillas developing into a regular army to achieve a conventional military victory.

Nasution and Simatupang planned a total popular defence, with the division of the *TNI* into 'Territorial' and 'Mobile' troops in a structure modelled on the German Wehrkreise system. For local defence, Territorial military 'pockets' would be established in the areas occupied by the Dutch, based on village networks. Here guerrilla commanders would function alongside parallel administrative structures, preserving a shadow Republican administration. Meanwhile, the *TNI* Mobile troops would conduct operations against economic and military targets, carrying out hit-and-run attacks on occupied towns and lines of communication. The Mobile troops' ratio of men to weapons was 1:1, while the Territorials could hope for only 1:3 or 1:5. Divisions were reduced from seven to four on Java and from four to one on Sumatra. The operational commands

Komando Jawa and *Komando Sumatera*, headed by Cols Nasution and Simatupang respectively, were set up for coordination.

In the event, the improved efficiency sought by the *RERA* programme was never achieved. The setting-up of the 'Wehrkreise' was delayed, instructions not being sent out until early November 1948. The reorganization of the units also failed: commanders formed as many theoretically Mobile battalions as possible, to the detriment of the planned Territorials. At the turn of 1948/49 the distinction between the two types of units had to be abandoned in the face of the successful Dutch Operation 'Crow', and the planned concentrated attacks virtually never happened.

Divided character

Within the Republican forces three distinct groups were identifiable: *laskar* non-state armed groups; ex-Japanese auxiliaries of the Giyûgun and Heiho; and ex-KNIL personnel (before the 1942 defeat the KNIL had been 80 per cent Indonesian, including a small number of trained officers). Former KNIL officers dominated the GHQ, while most unit commanders in the field were ex-Giyûgun. This led to vertical conflicts; in East and Central Java the GHQ could not assert itself effectively, and superior orders were routinely disregarded.

The ex-Giyûgun officers formed the backbone of the Republican army, which was thus dominated by Javanese officers with Java-centric attitudes. This Japanese-trained officer corps had been formed territorially, and consequently had mastered only small-unit – at most, battalion – tactics. Any higher military education was the preserve of the ex-KNIL officers, giving rise to the tensions between the senior command echelon and local commanders.

Equipment and training

The armament of the Republican army and the non-state armed groups was diverse, but

April 1946: this pilot of the *Angkatan Udara Republik Indonesia (AURI)* has just landed at Kemayoran airfield, Jakarta. He wears what looks like an Imperial Japanese Navy Type 3 flying helmet with hard earphones, Imperial Japanese Army winter flying overalls, and a Type 92 parachute. The aircraft is an IJA Type 99 Tachikawa Ki-55 ('Ida') advanced trainer. The *AURI*'s early wing marking was a disc halved red and white. (IPPHOS, 0086)

mainly comprised captured or surrendered Japanese weapons and pre-war KNIL stocks previously confiscated by the Japanese. It initially included not only small arms but also some artillery and light armour, but most of these were lost in 1945–46. Cut off from regular supplies of arms and ammunition from abroad, the nationalists had to rely very largely on captures from the Dutch, which were only sporadic. As a result, shortage of weapons and ammunition, and of means of communication, were the Achilles heels of the Indonesian armed struggle.

In December 1948, according to Dutch intelligence, only 40 to 50 per cent of the *TNI* on Java were armed, and on Sumatra about 25 per cent. A Sumatran battalion of 800–900 men had only 100–200 rifles or carbines, 4–6 light machine guns, and 1 or 2 heavy machine guns and mortars. Artillery was now limited to a section of two pieces in one regiment. Ammunition was often limited, and communications relied on civilian telephones or couriers. Moreover, individual and unit combat training was often rudimentary.

The combat value of the Republican army was not highly regarded by the Dutch, partly due to its shortage of armament. The Dutch commander, LtGen Spoor – who had made a career in the KNIL, and was not free from colonial prejudices – did not consider Gen Sudirman's forces to be a true 'army', but more a politico-military structure to coordinate various armed groups.

Strength

In November 1946 an Indonesian division consisted (on paper) of two to four brigades, each of two to three regiments, each of three to four battalions. In practical terms of organization and armament the brigades and divisions did not live up to their nominal designations, and their strengths differed enormously. For instance, in 1946 the I Div was estimated by the British at 43,155 men, and the V Div at 10,000. The divisions on Sumatra were all weaker, with strengths of 4,700 to 8,700 men. The estimated strength in that period was 118,155 men on Java and 41,800 men on Sumatra, a total of 159,955 (excluding *laskar* non-state groups).

Air Force and Navy

The Air Force, *Angkatan Udara Republik Indonesia (AURI)*, consisted of a few seized Japanese aircraft: initially two fighters, three light bombers, four transports, and a number of trainer types. On 9 April 1946 it became an independent branch of the armed forces, but it suffered from serious personnel and matériel shortages. There were few experienced pilots or

Java:
General Headquarters (Yogyakarta)
1 Regt MP, 2 Regt MP, 3 Regt MP
West Java:
I Div Siliwangi:
I Bde (1 & 2 Regts); II Bde (3, 4 & 5 Regts);
III Bde (6 & 7 Regts); IV Bde (8, 9 & 10 Regts)
II Div Sunan Gunung Jati:
V Bde (12, 13 & 14 Regts); VI Bde (15 & 16 Regts)
Central Java:
III Div Diponegoro:
VII Bde (17 & 18 Regts); VIII Bde (19 & 20 Regts);
IX Bde (21 & 22 Regts)
IV Div Penembahan Senopati: 23, 24, 25, 26 & 27 Regts
V Div Ronggolawe: 28, 29, 30 & 31 Regts
East Java:
VI Div Norotomo: 32, 33, 34 & 35 Regts
VII Div Surapati: 38, 39 & 40 Regts

Sumatra:
General HQ (Prapat & Bukittingi)
South Sumatra:
VIII Div Garuda:
X Bde (11, 12, 13, 14, 15, 16 & 17 Regts);
X Regt Marines
Central Sumatra:
IX Div Banteng:
XI Bde (1, 2, 3 & 4 Regts)
1 & 2 Regts *Tapanuli*, 3 Regt *Tapanuli* (forming),
4 Regt *Tapanuli;* Regt Marines
North Sumatra:
X Div Gadjah:
XII Bde (1, 2 & 3 Aceh Regts; 1, 2 & 3 East
Coast Regts; 3 Regt Marines)
Regt Artillery (?), Regt Engineers (?)

maintenance personnel, and a lack of spare parts. During Op 'Product' in July–August 1947, the Dutch destroyed 24 aircraft on the ground. They estimated that in 1948 the *AURI* had a maximum of 10 operational aircraft, and its roughly 6,000 personnel included only some 25 pilots.

The Republican Navy, *Angkatan Laut Republik Indonesia (ALRI)*, formed a modest force with a few small vessels and a few battalions for land combat. Its strength was estimated by the Dutch at 15,000 men.

Laskar non-state armed groups

In parallel to the *TRI/TNI*, numerous irregular or non-state armed groups, popularly termed *laskar,* operated independently. In September–October 1945 many 'revolutionary youth' had united in *Badan Perjuangan* ('combat groups'). These had both a political and a military character, some having been trained by the Japanese. Important examples were the socialist *Pesindo (Pemoeda Sosialis Indonesia);* the Islamic *Hizbullah;* and the *Laskar Boeroeh,* a trades-union federation. Additional independent armed

In 1945 a modest naval force was also formed, originally titled the *BKR Laut/TKR Laut* and later the *ALRI.* It had only a few small vessels, and most of the personnel served in land battalions. This August 1946 photo shows RI-408 *Gajah Muda* ('Young Elephant'), the *ALRI* flagship; it would be sunk off Cirebon by the Netherlands Royal Navy on 5 January 1947. (IPPHOS, 1930)

groups, arising mostly from youth organizations, included the *Barisan Banteng* ('Wild Buffalo Corps') and the *Laskar Rakjat* ('People's Militia').

The non-state groups were themselves divided by intense rivalries, over both their politics and their competition for scarce funding and weapons. The Republican government was faced with internal opposition from socialist or communist-oriented armed groups on the one hand, and Islamic groups on the other. The Republican military saw such groups as competitors, and tried to disarm or absorb them;

Eight *laskar* of a non-state armed group pose for the camera. One (rear left) wears camouflage overalls, presumably captured from the Dutch, while the others are all in mixed civilian and military clothing, and none display any insignia. Most such groups were short of weapons. Four of these men are armed with handguns: two with revolvers, and one with a Mauser C96 semi-automatic, of which the KNIL had received nearly 2,400 from China in 1941. Two of these irregulars have locally-made Japanese *shin-gunto* swords. (KTOMM Bronbeek, 2008/01/17-1-1/77)

opposition was often determined, and if persuasion failed then the *TRI/TNI* did not hesitate to apply lethal force.

In the January 1946 reorganization, the 'People's Militia' were nominally subordinated to the Ministry of Defence, but in fact they survived in parallel. Under the May 1947 reorganization plan the *laskar* were ordered integrated into *TNI* regiments and brigades, with mixed results. In 1948, in Surakarta and Madiun, left-wing forces united into the *FDR* (*Front Demokrasi Rakjat*; 'People's Democratic Front'), led by former defence minister and prime minister Amir Syarifuddin, and supported by the army's IV Div *Senopati*. The *FDR* clashed with the new right-wing Republican government; opposition to demobilizations broke out into open revolt, but this Madiun Rebellion was soon ruthlessly suppressed by the I Div *Siliwangi*.

The *Hizbullah* ('Army of Allah') was founded in December 1944 by an Islamic organization, *Masyumi*, but after the declaration of independence it developed separately as a military organization, growing to a strength of at least 20,000. Another Islamic militia, *Sabilillah* ('Warriors of Allah') appeared at the end of 1945, and both groups were known for their fanaticism.

Under the Renville Agreement in early 1948, the *TNI* withdrew from West Java into Central Java, but both Islamic groups stayed behind, merging into the *Tentara Islam Indonesia* (*TII*, 'Islamic Army of Indonesia'). In early 1949 the *TNI* returned to West Java, and confrontation with the *TII* became inevitable after the proclamation of a *Negara Islam Indonesia* ('Islamic State of Indonesia') on 7 August 1949. Years of internal conflict followed.

Dutch intelligence estimated the armament of the non-state groups at between 25 and 50 per cent, and due to their lack of funds they often lived at the expense of local populations. In addition to politically motivated groups, straightforward criminal gangs were also active.

DUTCH FORCES

Organization

Before World War II the Netherlands Indies had been defended by the Koninklijk Nederlands–Indisch Leger (Royal Netherlands Indies Army, KNIL) and the Koninklijke Marine (Netherlands Royal Navy, KM). For the reoccupation these were reinforced by the Dutch metropolitan Koninklijke Landmacht (Royal Army, KL). Both armies needed complete reconstruction after World War II, and both largely followed British organizational models.

While ultimate political decisions were taken by the government and parliament at The Hague in the Netherlands, in the Indies the lieutenant governor-general (from 1948, Crown high commissioner) was both the civil representative of the Dutch state and the commander-in-chief of the Army and Navy (though these had no joint headquarters). An integrated civil/military command structure for co-ordinating the operations of the civil service, police and military was discussed, but in the end it was never established. The civil service and police were too weak to enjoy equivalence with the armed forces, and were forced into subordinate roles.

At the head of the KNIL's Algemeen Hoofdkwartier (General Headquarters, AHK) was the KNIL army commander, with authority over all KNIL and KL troops in the Netherlands Indies; from January 1946 this appointment was held by LtGen Simon Hendrik Spoor. The other senior staff positions were also held by KNIL officers, as usually were those in operational brigades.

During the conflict the KNIL thus determined not only doctrine and strategy, but also the operational and tactical deployments of both colonial and metropolitan troops. The main theatre of operations in Java and Sumatra was divided into dual 'territorial & troop commands' (TTCs), where divisional and some brigade staffs were charged with the parallel tasks of territorial security and manoeuvre operations.

Formations

During 1946, Dutch units and formations took over from the British on Java and Sumatra. The initially autonomous KL battalions, together with KNIL units, were grouped into seven brigades designated in-country as T, U, V, W, X, Y and Z Brigades. On Java, these brigades (each about 3,500 strong) came under two to three divisional HQs: those of A Div, were in Surabaya, and B Div in Bandung. Divisional troops consisted of an HQ, divisional signals, a tank squadron, field artillery battery, and support services. In 1946 a brigade comprised an HQ, three infantry battalions and one of artillery, a reconnaissance squadron, engineer company, signals company, medical company, motor transport company, and repair company.

During 1946 conscripts of the KL's 1st Div '7 December', and in early 1947 of 2nd Div, were sent out as reinforcements, being redesignated in-country as C Div '7 December' and D Division. The former was

Simon Hendrik Spoor was a member of the 1923 promotion from the Royal Military Academy (KMA). In 1929–32, he studied at the War College, and himself taught tactics and strategy at the KMA in 1934–38. Evacuated to Australia in 1942, he became head of the Netherlands Forces Intelligence Service. Back on Java, the 44-year-old Spoor was appointed army commander in the Indies on 19 January 1946, with the temporary rank of lieutenant-general. Although he lacked operational experience above company level, he was a skilled intelligence and staff officer, dedicated and hard-working, and he earned the devotion of his men. (KTOMM Bronbeek, 1971-01-15-5)

A Dutch infantry patrol in section (squad) strength in position along the edge of a track, during the advance of X Bde from the Surabaya perimeter over the mountains to Malang in late July 1947. A ten-man section consisted of a Bren gun group of a corporal and two men, and a rifle group of a sergeant and six men. These soldiers wear US olive-drab field caps and 1942 camouflage overalls (see Plate E). Two carry British Ptn 08/37 webbing 'large packs', and the foreground soldier has a machine in a scabbard. (KTOMM Bronbeek, 2008/01/17-1-1/79)

deployed entirely in West Java, and the three brigades of D Div separately in East Java, South Sumatra and North Sumatra. The two KL light infantry divisions comprised three brigades, plus combat support and services units. Both the KL and KNIL also raised territorial second-line 'guards duties' units termed Bewakingsbataljons. (For examples of all the above, see July 1947 order of battle on page 37, and abbreviations on page 2.) No other operational division was formed from the 1947 conscript class, but 15 separate infantry battalions and combat support units were sent out under the collective administrative identity 'E Division'. During 1948 the system changed, to forming and deploying every six months an Independent Infantry Brigade (Zelfstandige Infanteriebrigade, ZIB) plus three battalions outside this structure. Before the transfer of sovereignty in December 1949 three ZIBs had been deployed, designated in-country as F, G and H Brigades.

Due to the local conditions, it was usually neither possible nor necessary to operate at a divisional echelon (except during the two main offensives, Operations 'Product' and 'Crow'). Divisional staffs otherwise limited themselves to the preparation of smaller operations, while providing territorial command structures. The brigades were made self-sufficient by the addition of combat support and services elements.

Strengths

By the end of 1946 the in-country strengths of the KNIL and KL were around 55,000 and 41,000 respectively. The KL overtook the KNIL in about February 1947, and by the end of that year had some 79,000 men to just under 60,000 KNIL. This ratio was little changed at the end of 1948, the total still standing at around 140,000. Peak strength reached approximately 148,000 in mid-1949.

In 1948 in particular there was a serious shortage of infantry, which became even more dire in 1949. After three years of service, the first KL units were eligible for repatriation; the KNIL also faced the demobilization of conscripts and recuperation leave for its regular personnel; and the Marine Brigade had to be steadily reduced. Solutions were sought in the postponement of repatriations, and the establishment of new local units.

KONINKLIJK NEDERLANDS-INDISCH LEGER (KNIL)
Organization

After the Japanese surrender the reborn Royal Netherlands-Indies Army proceeded to form 23 infantry battalions from ex-POWs, reservists and new recruits; from 1946 battalion organization generally mirrored that in the KL (see below). The additional combat support units formed would be three field artillery battalions; four tank squadrons; four engineer field companies and six labour companies; five second-line 'guard duty' (Bewakings) battalions; a general transport company; nine general hospitals, and a military police corps.

The KNIL also formed paratroop and commando elements. On 1 March 1946 a Paratroop Training School (SOP) was established, and later in 1947 this formed an operational 267-strong 1st Parachute Company (Para 1). A commando-training Special Forces Depot (DST) was established on 15 June 1946; renamed in August 1948 the Special Forces Corps (KST), this also formed a parachute company (Para KST). These two companies were operationally united into a Para Combat Group. On 15 July 1949 the SOP, Para 1 and KST were disbanded and replaced by the Special Forces Regt (RST), with a parachute battalion (RST-I) and a commando battalion (RST-II), totalling about 1,250 men. The paratroopers and commandos were often deployed as 'fire brigades', and were known for their aggressive character.

Composition

The KNIL based its manpower on contract (volunteer) soldiers, both Indonesian and Dutch. However, it additionally drew upon Netherlands-resident conscripts and reserve officers who had been called up during the mobilization of December 1941; these were asked in 1945 to sign up for another year. In the event, it was not until 1948 that some 5,900 conscripts and reserve officers were able to go on extended leave.

1949: paratroopers of the KNIL's Special Forces Regt (RST) ready for a practice jump from a C-47 'Dakota'. The paratroopers wear jungle-green uniform, while the despatcher has camouflage overalls with US canvas leggings (see Plate F). The equipment is mixed British and American: the parachutes are wartime Irvin rigs, the man at the left has the British despatch rider's steel helmet, and the man in the door a US 1937 tank helmet and M1943 'double-buckle' boots. (NIMH, 2155_023662)

In the multi-ethnic KNIL the officers were predominantly Dutch, and the rank-and-file mainly Indonesian around a core of Dutch and Eurasians (i.e. mixed-race personnel). During 1945–48 the Dutch share was relatively higher than the pre-war norm, mainly due to the inaccessibility of important recruitment areas on Sumatra and Java. Indonesian recruits were disproportionately from ethnic minority groups which were deemed more loyal to the colonial state – Ambonese, Manadonese, Keiese and Timorese, and new groups such as Torajas from Sulawesi. These partly Christian minorities had traditionally acted as a counterweight to the mainly Muslim Javanese. On 1 December 1949 the KNIL numbered 66,621 men, of whom 51,043 were Indonesians.

Enlistment was based on a renewable short-term contract of one year. The infantry battalions were organized in multi-ethnic mixed companies or, as before World War II, in single-ethnic companies. In a mixed company Indonesian soldiers served together regardless of individual origin, but in a single-ethnic company they were all from the same background. European and mixed-race soldiers served together in Dutch companies. In 1945/46 a new generation of officers arrived, who had been captains when evacuated to Australia before the defeat of March 1942. Now they passed over many higher-ranking officers returning from captivity, and many of the latter, aged 50 or over, were retired.

The head of a combat patrol, probably from II-15 RI, during the pacification phase in East Java, 1948–49. Minimum patrol strength was an eight-man section with at least one automatic weapon. The NCO patrol leader is armed with a Sten Mk 2 sub-machine gun; he is followed by the Bren gunner, for instant firepower in case of a contact, and then by at least six riflemen. For uniform, see Plate E. (KTOMM Bronbeek, 2013/06/01-3-2/47)

In order to relieve the KL and KNIL of static security tasks, a start was made at the end of 1947 in forming additional territorial KNIL 'security' battalions. About 11 were established under various names in 1948–49, primarily to maintain law and order in their own areas.

As part of the preparations for the planned federation, the name of the KNIL was changed on 1 September 1948 to Royal Netherlands-Indonesian Army, with the abbreviation unchanged.

General Spoor saw a leading role for the KNIL in the new armed forces of federal Indonesia in the service of a Dutch-Indonesian Union, but the Republic thought otherwise. While absorbing large numbers of KNIL personnel, its own *TNI* would form the new Indonesian army after the transfer of sovereignty in 1949, and the KNIL was dissolved on 26 July 1950. By the end of October 1950, 25,850 men had been transferred as formed units or individuals to the Indonesian armed forces; 25,602 had been demobilized, and 6,250 had left for the Netherlands, leaving 7,258 still awaiting settlement.

Militaire Luchtvaart (ML-KNIL)

The KNIL's aviation branch contributed eight-plus squadrons:

    16 & 18 Sqns (North American B-25 Mitchell medium bombers)
    120 Sqn (Curtiss P-40N Kittyhawk fighters)
    121 & 122 Sqns (North American P-51D & K Mustang fighters)
    19 Sqn (Douglas C-47 'Dakota' transports)
    20 Sqn (B-25 Mitchell transports)
    17 Sqn, VARWA (Piper L-4J Cub recon & artillery obs aircraft)
    Photo Recon Unit, PVA (B-25 Mitchells)

Operational deployments were hindered by shortages of trained personnel and spare parts. Some ML-KNIL aircraft had been in use since 1942/43, but there were financial and political constraints on purchasing replacements.

KONINKLIJKE LANDMACHT (KL)
Composition

The Royal Army had mixed manpower based on conscription around a small professional cadre of volunteers and mobilized reservists. 'War volunteers' were also recruited between autumn 1944 and August 1946, when enlistment of these Oorlogsvrijwilliger ('OVW-ers') was discontinued, and most of them were demobilized in 1948.

Male Dutch nationals and other residents of the country aged 18 to 40 or 45 were conscripted for a period of compulsory military service that was set in 1947 at 11 to 15 months. It was extended in 1948 to 12 to 24 months, but for conscripts on active service overseas the duration could be extended by an additional 6 to 12 months. Under the Dutch

(continued on page 29)

THE *BERSIAP*, 1945
1: *Pemuda*
2: *Pemudi, BPRI*
3: *Pemuda, Tentara Peladjar*

REPUBLICAN POLICE & ARMY, 1946–49
1: *Komisaris kl I*, Republican police, 1948
2: *Sersan kl II, TRI*, 1946–47
3: *Major, TNI*, 1949
4: *TRI* divisional flag

B

REPUBLICAN NAVY & AIR FORCE
1: *Pradjurit II, ALRI,* 1946
2: *Tjalon Letnan, ALRI*
3: *Kadet Udara I, AURI*
4: Alternative *ALRI* officers' ranking

ROYAL NETHERLANDS–INDIES FORCES, 1946–49
1: Ambonese infantryman, KNIL
2: Korporaal, VK-KNIL
3: Onderluitenant pilot, ML-KNIL

2

2a

1

3

D

NETHERLANDS ROYAL ARMY, 1947–48
1: Soldaat 1ste klasse, 7 Regiment Infanterie
2: Majoor, Regt Huzaren van Boreel
3: Infantry Bren-gunner

E

**NETHERLANDS ROYAL NAVY, KNIL PARATROOPS
& SPECIAL FORCES**
1: Sergeant, KM, 1945
2: KNIL paratrooper, SOP, 1947
2a: Metal sleeve badge, SOP
3: KNIL commando, DST, 1948
3a: Metal sleeve badge, DST

F

KM MARBRIG, & MARVA
1: BAR gunner, Marine infantry
2: Marine tank crewman
3: MARVA 1ste klasse

CIVIL SERVICE, GENERAL POLICE, & PAT
1: Controleur 1ste klasse, 1946–49
2: Commissaris 2de klasse, Algemene Politie, 1947
3: Chinese volunteer, Pao An Tui, 1947
3a: PAT cap badge

constitution KL conscripts initially could not be sent to the colonies without their agreement; in 1946, however, the constitution was amended to remove this protection, although their overseas posting should last no later than the end of 1949. In practice, a posting to the Indies usually lasted at least three years.

Conscripts were called up annually and, from 1948, every six months. Basic training lasted 6–12 weeks, followed by a variable period of advanced specialist training, and 4–6 weeks of in-unit training. Operational battalions were formed from training units, being disbanded when the conscripts were demobilized. This system ensured that a soldier served with the same comrades and leaders throughout his training and active service, with obvious benefits for unit cohesion.

The rifle group within a KNIL infantry section, wearing Dutch jungle-green battledress with British Ptn 37 web equipment, and armed with Lee Enfield No. 4 rifles. The section commander (left) is a European sergeant; his rank insignia, a brass plate with a blue stripe, is just visible on his collar point. The riflemen are of mixed Indonesian ethnic groups. (KTOMM Bronbeek, 2008/01/17-1-1/47)

Battalion organization

In 1945 the KL sent out to the Indies light-infantry battalions (LIBs), formed from its then only available manpower of 'OVW-ers'. Originally intended for occupation duty in West Germany, they had an establishment of 801 in a battalion HQ, HQ company (without heavy weapons), and five rifle companies. They proved too lightly armed, sketchily trained, and lacking in transport for operations in the Indies. Fully-equipped and trained infantry battalions were needed, brigaded with supporting elements such as artillery battalions, tank squadrons, engineer and transport companies.

From the turn of 1945/46 the LIBs in-country were therefore reorganized, and stronger infantry battalions on the British model, composed of both 'OVW-ers' and conscripts, were shipped to the Indies between mid-1946 and early 1947. Their establishment was 845 (37 officers, 89 NCOs and 719 other ranks), organized in a battalion HQ, HQ company, four rifle companies and a support company. Apart from small arms and 63 Bren light machine guns, each had 23 PIAT anti-tank projectors, 26x 2in and 6x 3in mortars, and 6x 6-pdr anti-tank guns. The

This North American B-25J-15 Mitchell, with a solid nose mounting eight .50-cal machine guns for strafing, served with the ML-KNIL's 18 Sqn , based at the end of 1945 at Nr. 1 Air Base (1 VB) Cililitan, south-east of Jakarta in West Java. The squadron had both solid-nose and bomb-aimer nose B-25s on strength. Numbered M-433, this Mitchell would be handed over to the Indonesian *AURI* in 1950. (KTOMM Bronbeek, 1995/10/18-2/41)

battalion's official scale of transport was 33 bicycles, 27 motorcycles, a four-seat car, 11 jeeps, 27x ¾-ton trucks, 7 Loyd and 19 Universal tracked carriers, and a ¾-ton 180-gal water trailer.

Equipment

The German and Japanese occupations had ruined the economies of both the Netherlands and the Indies. The equipment, armament and maintenance of the KL and KNIL therefore presented major challenges, and the Netherlands – like Indonesia – fought a 'poor man's war'. British, Canadian and Australian equipment was acquired, much of it from surplus stocks in Europe, India and the Pacific, and some supplied directly by the Australian and British Indian armies. In some units weapons had to be augmented with Japanese and pre-war KNIL types.

The standard small arms of the KL and KNIL were the British .303in Lee Enfield No. 4 bolt-action rifle, the 9mm Sten sub-machine gun, and, as the section weapon, the .303in Bren light machine gun. At platoon and battalion level respectively the British 2in and 3in mortars were deployed, the latter alongside .303in Vickers medium machine guns. The KL field artillery was armed with the British 25-pdr (3.45in/87.6mm) quick-firing gun-howitzer towed by the Morris C8 tractor. The KNIL field artillery had the shortened 'break-down' version of the 25-pdr, provided by the Australian Army.

American and British vehicles included jeeps, GMC trucks, Dodge weapons-carriers, and Universal and Loyd tracked carriers. The armoured car squadrons had the Humber Mk IV, the Humber Mk II scout car, and the Canadian C15TA armoured 15-cwt (¾-ton) truck. The reconnaissance squadrons had Ford Lynx Mk II scout cars, C15TAs, and Hum-Fox armoured cars (a Canadian design modified with the 37mm-gun turret of the Humber Mk IV). Tank units had Stuart light tanks handed over by the British Indian Army: 38x M3A3s, 4x M3A5s, and 12x turretless M3A5s.

Some local irregulars also fought as scouts on the Dutch side, although the high command regarded them with suspicion. From 1947 the intelligence officer of 3rd Bn, 9 Inf Regt (III-9 RI), a unit of KL conscripts, employed defected *laskar*. They were often from gangs active south of Jakarta; the photo was taken at Krawang, West Java during 1947. Known as 'Her Majesty's Irregular Troops' (HAMOT), their strength fluctuated between 75 and 120 men. They were later assigned to the KNIL battalion Inf XX as its 4th 'Skirmish' Company. (NIMH, 2000-1368-05)

Militaire Luchtvaart (ML)

Unofficially known as the Legerluchtmacht (Army Air Force), this corps provided, during 1946 and the second half of 1947, the following assets:

  6 Sqn, ARVA (Auster Mk II recon & artillery obs aircraft)
  322 Sqn (Spitfire Mk IX fighters)
  Four companies of airfield defence troops (Luchtvaarttroepen).

KONINKLIJKE MARINE (KM)
Marine Brigade

In 1943 it was decided to create a reinforced regiment of 'Free' Netherlands Royal Navy marines for the war against Japan. Comprising both professionals and 'war volunteers', this was trained and equipped in the United States. As the Marine Brigade, it was transferred to the Netherlands Indies in November 1945, being deployed exclusively in East Java. It had an initial establishment of 6,344 all ranks, organized in a brigade staff, three infantry battalions, a heavy weapons company, artillery battalion, engineer battalion, tank company, reconnaissance company, amphibious tractor ('amtrac') company, and service troops. During late 1947–early 1948 the brigade was reduced to a regiment of

KM marines in action on 22 June 1946 in the enclave around Surabaya, against a background of burning houses. Offensive action outside the perimeter was officially forbidden, despite Indonesian shelling and attacks on posts, but there was reciprocal patrol activity. All these men seem to be armed with the American M1 carbine. (NIMH, 2174-0259)

Seen in Malang during a pause in Operation 'Product/South' in July 1947, this Sherman M4A3 is number 'A2', serial 'P3365', and is named 'Harssens'. Mounting a 105mm howitzer, it served in A Platoon of the KM Marine Brigade's Tankco. (NIMH, 2174-0842)

4,350 men, the original 'war volunteers' being steadily replaced by conscripts (Zeemiliciens). A further reduction to a 1,200-strong reinforced amphibious battalion followed in early 1949.

The KM's Marbrig, with its brand-new American kit, was the best-equipped element of the Dutch forces. Standard weapons were the semi-automatic .30-cal M1 Garand rifle, the 'short .30-cal' M1 carbine, and generous numbers of the .30-cal M1918A2 Browning Automatic Rifle (BAR). Crew-served weapons were the .30-cal M1919 medium machine gun, .50-cal M2 heavy machine gun, and 81mm M1 mortar. The reconnaissance company had M8 light armoured cars and M3A1 half-tracks, and the tank company M4A3 Shermans. The artillery battalion established in Surabaya in early 1946 had British-supplied 25-pdrs and Morris tractors.

In addition to the Marbrig, the KM provided assets for sea transport, amphibious landings, and naval gunfire support, and was also deployed to monitor shipping traffic. After the British departure the KM focused on coastal surveillance around Java and Sumatra, to prevent Republican arms imports and infiltrations, smuggling and piracy. This blockade, carried out by dozens of mostly small vessels with air support from the MLD, was relatively successful.

Marine Luchtvaart Afdeling (MLD)

The Naval Air Service operated two squadrons in the Indies:

> 321 Sqn, reorganized 28 February 1946 into Oosterlijk Verkennings- en Transport Sqn, OVTS (12 Consolidated PBY Catalina flying boats & 15 C-47 'Dakota' transports). Reverted to 321 Sqn, 1 May 1949.
>
> 860 Sqn (15 Fairey Firefly Mk IV fighters).

THE COURSE OF THE WAR

Dutch strategy

Recolonization was initially seen by the senior military commanders in the Indies purely in terms of security, and they considered a military reoccupation, beginning with Java, both desirable and possible. However, Lieutenant Governor-General Van Mook recognized the actual balance of power, and insisted on negotiations with the Republic. While agreeing that military action on Java was necessary in order to put pressure on the nationalists, he also favoured an 'Outer Regions first' strategy. The hardliners were replaced, and LtGen Simon Hendrik Spoor was appointed KNIL army commander on 1 February 1946.

After East Indonesia and Dutch Borneo (the 'Outer Regions') had been brought under control, the focus would be on the reconquest of Java and Sumatra. General Spoor planned to achieve this by a 'spearhead strategy', in which he distinguished five phases:

Operational phases:

1st phase: penetration of the enemy resistance zone.

2nd phase: pushing into the enemy's rear area to occupy important tactical and economic objectives.

3rd phase: the decisive battle, followed by occupying the heart of the country.

Pacification phases:

4th phase: securing, and then extending, captured objectives and communications.

5th phase: rendering harmless remaining hostile elements, and countering infiltration.

During the operational phases, fast mobile columns were to penetrate deeply into enemy territory, eliminate the enemy leadership and occupy important positions. The core of the combat columns would be infantry, ranging from company to brigade strength, reinforced with artillery, armour, engineer and transport units. The ML-KNIL and MLD would provide air support, reconnaissance, and possibly re-supply to these combat columns, and the KM, sea transport and naval gunfire support. After the operational phases, the pacification phases would eliminate the remaining enemy by dispersing Dutch units over each area to be mopped up, and aggressive patrolling. However, the expectation was that only in the dry season (May–June) of 1947 would the three divisions deemed necessary be available for the large-scale 3rd-phase offensive, so the military build-up for this would take more than a year.

The government publicly presented their military activity as 'security operations' rather than a war, and the two major offensives would officially be called 'police actions'. Although there were very significant differences from the contemporaneous French situation in Indochina, the Dutch, like the French, fundamentally misjudged the opposition they faced. They believed that only a minority of the population – mainly the young, and the intelligentsia – would support the Republic, while the great majority would welcome the stability of restored colonial rule. The elimination of its leadership and its main armed elements would therefore lead to the collapse of the decapitated insurgency. This misjudgement gave birth to a purely military and punitive approach,

During the unrest in Jakarta after the Japanese capitulation, a KNIL patrol searches an Indonesian. The liberated POWs, of various ethnic groups, have armed themselves with (left to right) a .45cal American Thompson sub-machine gun, a 9mm Australian Austen SMG, and a Dutch M95 carbine. The right-hand soldier also has a pre-war KNIL helmet, pouch and *klewang*. (IWM SE 5734)

On 28 October 1945, nationalist mobs and *TKR* personnel attacked 49th Indian Inf Bde in Surabaya. This photo of Indonesian fighters was taken on 10 November, the first day of the bloody fighting to recapture the city by reinforcements from 5th Indian Infantry Division. Other photos of the time show Indonesians armed with Japanese and Dutch weapons, such as the 6.5mm Type 11 (1922) light machine gun, and the pre-war KNIL's 9mm Schmeisser MP28/II, while a few have Japanese or KNIL helmets. (IPPHOS, 0035)

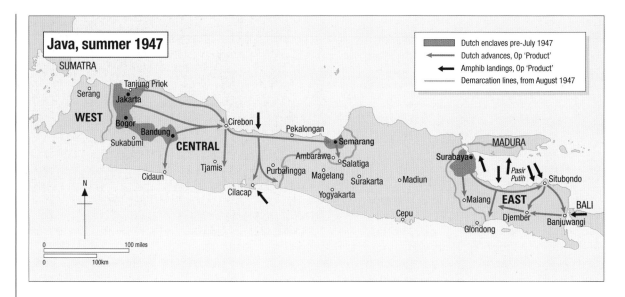

Java, summer 1947

SUMATRA

Dutch enclaves pre-July 1947
Dutch advances, Op 'Product'
Amphib landings, Op 'Product'
Demarcation lines, from August 1947

Serang
Tanjung Priok
Jakarta
WEST
Bogor
Bandung
Sukabumi
CENTRAL
Cidaun
Tjamis
Cilacap
Cirebon
Pekalongan
Semarang
Ambarawa
Salatiga
Purbalingga
Magelang
Surakarta
Madiun
Yogyakarta
Cepu
MADURA
Surabaya
Pasir Putih
Situbondo
Malang
EAST
BALI
Djember
Banjuwangi
Glondong

N

0   100 miles
0   100km

For reasons of space, we have chosen to include only this sketch map of Operation 'Product' on Java in summer 1947. In MAA 521, *Royal Netherlands East Indies Army 1936–42*, pages 34–35, readers will find a map of the whole Indonesian archipelago and adjoining territories in 1942.

focusing on territorial control, to what was a much wider socio-political challenge; consequently, eventual failure was inevitable.

The *Bersiap*, 1945

In the weeks after the Japanese capitulation Java remained mainly quiet under continuing Japanese control, but this changed with the arrival of British Indian troops and the NICA at the end of September 1945. Recognized as heralding the colonizers' return, this provoked an outburst of violence by nationalist armed groups, mostly of young people, sometimes supported by Republican military personnel. This period is known in the Netherlands as the *Bersiap*, an Indonesian term meaning 'be ready'. The extreme violence expressed opposition to the return of the colonial regime, but also popular hatred against the former political, social and ethnic elites. Europeans and Eurasians, Ambonese, Chinese, and also members of the old Indonesian administrative nobility, all fell victim to mass terrorism, and some consequently took up arms for self-protection and revenge. It is estimated that perhaps 6,000 people were killed before the violence began to peter out at the beginning of 1946.

Battle for the cities, 1945–46

In November–December 1945, armed confrontations for control of the cities broke out between mostly British Indian troops (plus small numbers of liberated KNIL personnel), and Indonesian nationalists seeking to occupy Jakarta, Bandung, Semarang and Surabaya. Often the Indonesians employed 'human wave' tactics, sometimes advancing behind human shields; these attacks were defeated with heavy casualties, and the loss of most of their Japanese heavy weapons.

In East and Central Java the fighting started in late October. After a local Japanese surrender at Surabaya on 3 October, well-armed Indonesians were already in control of this East Javanese port when 49th Indian Inf Bde from 23rd Indian Inf Div came ashore on 25 October. A British attempt to disarm the Indonesians provoked a general attack on 28 October by the *TKR*, non-state groups and armed civilians. Despite a fragile truce reportedly reached with Soekarno's support, the British brigade commander was killed. Reinforced by part of 5th Indian Inf Div, the British reoccupied the city in weeks of heavy fighting between 10 and 29 November.

From Semarang, recaptured by Japanese troops, small British Indian detachments went inland to Ambarawa and Magelang. At the latter town, on 31 October the 3/10th Gurkha Rifles were attacked, and Japanese troops were deployed to reinforce them. Here too a truce was concluded, and the British cleared Magelang on 21 November. Heavy fighting resumed at Semarang on 18 November, but 23rd Div's artillery, air support and naval gunfire helped to retrieve the situation. The Indonesians attacked Ambarawa on 20 November; after RAF air support and re-supply, the garrison retreated to Semarang on 14 December 1945.

Now alerted to the true challenge, the British reinforced West Java. The cities of Jakarta, Bogor (Buitenzorg) and Bandung were successively purged and brought under control with a heavy hand. The vulnerable 130-mile route connecting these cities was initially secured by Japanese units including tanks. At the end of 1945 a KNIL 1st Inf Regt was deployed in and around Jakarta under British command. Established on 6 October 1945, this had three battalions (Inf I, Inf II & Inf IV), of which the first would soon be replaced with Inf V, raised in Bandung. The troops were mainly barely-recovered ex-POWs and young volunteers; they and their families had faced grave danger during the *Bersiap*, and they were consequently trigger-happy.

For Op 'Product' a tank squadron was attached to each of three brigades operating from Bandung and Semarang, and the Marine Bde deployed its integral squadron from Surabaya. The Dutch armour was normally dispersed between the enclaves in the infantry-support role, like this M3A3 Stuart leading a motorized column during 1947. The nationalists had very few anti-tank weapons, and the main threat was from improvised explosive devices or the frequent advance sabotage of roads and bridges. (NIMH, 2155_024461)

Outer Regions, 1945–46

In Balikpapan, SE Borneo, liberated KNIL prisoners were formed into infantry units and distributed over the Outer Regions. Outside of Sumatra and Java, Australian troops had occupied large areas from Borneo, which they had conquered from the Japanese. On 2 February 1946 AFNEI took over responsibility, and 80th Indian Inf Bde from 20th Indian Inf Div disembarked to replace the Australians at Makassar (South Sulawesi).

In general the Dutch takeover went relatively smoothly, but South Sulawesi was an exception. The Republican movement had widespread support there, and, although initially driven underground, the resistance increased in the second half of 1946, partly due to support from Java. Terror and counter-terror killed hundreds, and in December 1946 the colonial government declared a state of war in South Sulawesi. KNIL commandos from the Special Forces Depot were temporarily deployed there, commanded by Reserve 1st Lt Raymond Westerling. This officer applied extreme measures, including summary executions, and enforced active local cooperation. By the end of March 1947 he had achieved, if not true pacification, then at least obedience, at a reported cost of 5,182 deaths as a result of extrajudicial action by the DST, police and local

irregulars. On the other side, the number of local victims of the nationalist resistance is estimated at 1,500. According to the Indonesian Col Nasution, Westerling's actions successfully isolated the guerrillas from the population, both literally and psychologically, and thus neutralized them.

The enclaves and ceasefire, 1946–47

During 1946, Dutch troops took over the urban enclaves on Java and Sumatra from the British forces. These, and the roads linking them, were subject to frequent Indonesian fire including by artillery,

On 21 July 1947, during Op 'Product', two reinforced battalions of the KM Marbrig made an amphibious landing at Pasir Putih in East Java. After ten minutes of naval gunfire preparation and with air support from MLD fighters, the first wave, consisting of two reinforced platoons in four Landing Craft Personnel supported by two river patrol craft, headed for the beach, landing unopposed. (NIMH, 2174-0819)

and to large-scale infantry assaults on posts. Shortage of troops largely limited the Dutch to securing their perimeters, but they did make occasional sorties.

Under the auspices of the soon-to-depart British, an armistice was signed on 14 October 1946, and a month later the draft Linggarjati Agreement was concluded between Dutch and Republican envoys; this recognized *de facto* Republican authority over territory outside the Dutch enclaves, and hinted at the possibility of a peaceful outcome. However, this agreement soon stalled, and the armistice failed. The Indonesian C-in-C, Gen Sudirman, did not give orders to cease fire until 24 January 1947, and in the meantime Indonesian shelling and infiltrations continued along the disputed demarcation lines. Conversely, in East Java the Marine Bde expanded the enclave of Surabaya significantly in three actions in July 1946, January and March 1947.

Operation 'Product', 1947

The draft Linggarjati Agreement produced only political deadlock, while fighting continued despite the official ceasefire; between the start of 1946 and mid-1947, Dutch fatalities had been running at *c.* 260 per quarter. With a negative trade balance, the Netherlands was on the brink of bankruptcy, with huge dollar debts. In the Indies, Dutch authority was limited to a few enclaves without economic hinterland, and thus denied the income upon which the colonial government depended. The Dutch government decided to issue an ultimatum: if the Republic did not implement the Linggarjati Agreement, its terms would be enforced by military action. Despite their limited resources, the military leadership would have preferred a more ambitious plan, but, at the intercession of Lieutenant Governor-General Van Mook and the home government, they ultimately opted for a limited offensive to occupy parts of the Republican territory on Java and Sumatra mainly selected for their economic potential. Its objectives were as follows:
- Occupation of West Java, with the exception of the south-west; limited extension of perimeter around Semarang; occupation of Java's eastern extremity (the 'Oosthoek').
- Occupation of cultivated areas near Medan (North Sumatra) and on the Padang Plain (Central Sumatra); and of the oilfields and coalmines near Lahat (South Sumatra).

DUTCH ORDER OF BATTLE, JULY 1947

Note: Infantry units abbreviated e.g. I-5 RI, III RG, etc. were KL first-line battalions. The III & IV Bats of 3, 5, 7, 8 & 10 RI were second-line units (Bew Bats). KNIL first- and second-line units are abbreviated e.g. Inf V, and III Bew Bat, respectively. See also listed abbreviations on page 2.

General Headquarters
Military Police Corps

Territorial & Troop Command West Java
C Div '7 Dec', Jakarta: *1 Infbrig Gp* (III RG, III RJ, III RPI, IV-10 RI; I-2 RVA, III-2 RVA, 1-1 Verk R). *2 Infbrig Gp* (III-1 RI, III-9 RI, III-12 RI; I-6 RVA, II-6 RVA, 3-1 Verk R). *3 Infbrig Gp* (III RS, III-2 RI, III-14 RI; I-8 RVA, III-8 RVA, 2-1 Verk R), plus divisional troops
Local Command Batavia (III Bew Bat, IV-3 RI, IV-8 RI, IV-11 RI, III-10 RI, I Bew Bat)
B Div, Bandung: *V Brig* (I-3 RI, I-5 RI, I-9 RI, Inf V; 5 AVA, III-6 RVA, 4 Paw, Vew 2). *W Brig* (I-4 RI, II-4 RI, I-11 RI, Inf I; A III Veld, II-12 RVA, Vew 1), plus divisional troops
Local Command Bandung (II Bew Bat, III-8 RI, part IV-3 RI)

Territorial &Troop Command Central Java
T Brig (I RS, II-6 RI, II-7 RI, II-13 RI; A I Veld, 2 Paw, Vew 3)
Local Command Semarang (V Bew Bat, III-7 RI, IV RPI, IV-6 RI)

Territorial &Troop Command East Java
A Div, Surabaya: *1 Marbrig* (1, 2 & 3 INBAT, ARBAT, VERKA, TANKCO). *X Brig* (II-5 RI, I-12 RI, II-10 RI, III-5 RI, IV-5 RI; A II Veld). *4 Infbrig* (IV RJ, IV RG; I-12 RVA), plus divisional troops (Vew 4)

Territorial & Troop Command North Sumatra
Z Brig (Inf IV, Inf VI, I-1 RI, III-3 RI; 7 AVA, 9 AVA, 1 Paw). *6 Infbrig* (IV RS, IV-2 RI)
Troop Command Sabang (Inf III)

Territorial & Troop Command Central Sumatra
U Brig (I RJ, I-8 RI, II-14 RI; 4 AVA, 5 Paw)

Territorial &Troop Command South Sumatra
Y Brig (Inf X, Inf XI, VII RS, VIII RS; 6 AVA, 8 AVA, 3 Paw, 6 Paw). *5 Infbrig* (IV-1 RI, IV-4 RI, IV-7 RI)
Troop Command Bangka–Belitung (Inf VII)

Territorial & Troop Command East Indonesia
TTC Bali/Lombok (Inf XII)
TTC SE Borneo (Inf XIII, Inf XIV, Inf XXIII, 3-11 RI)
TTC West Borneo (Inf IX)
TTC North Sulawesi (Inf XVIII)
TTC South Sulawesi (Inf XV, Inf XVI, Inf XVII)
TTC New Guinea (Inf XX)
TTC Maluku (Inf XIX, Inf XXI)
TTC Riau (Inf VIII)

Air Command
18 Sqn, PVA, 19 Sqn, 20 Sqn
Regional Air Command Java
120 Sqn, 121 Sqn, 6 Sqn ARVA
Regional Air Command Sumatra
16 Sqn, 122 Sqn, 17 Sqn VARWA

Koninklijke Marine, NI
Destroyers: HNLMS *Piet Hein*, HNLMS *Evertsen*, HNLMS *Banckert*, HNLMS *Tjerk Hiddes*
Naval Commands
Surabaya, East Indonesia, Australia
Under senior officer present (OAZ):
Bali, Semarang, Tanjung Priok (Jakarta), Palembang, Belawan Deli
Small Vessel Service (KVD)
Patrol boats
Naval Aviation Service (MLD)
OVTS, 860 Sqn.

General Spoor aimed to achieve these goals by means of the 'spearhead strategy' described above. The operational phases were planned to last 14 days. No duration was set for the pacification phases, but some at AKH anticipated a success which would allow an overall force reduction in three to six months. General Spoor himself was less sanguine, believing that complete pacification and the elimination of guerrillas would probably take five years.

Operation 'Product' (officially, the 'First Police Action' in Dutch sources, and *Agresi Militer Belanda I*, 'First Dutch Military Aggression' in Indonesian), began on 20 July 1947. Due to a postponement, the element of surprise was partly lost. Dutch forces thrust out of the enclaves and penetrated the Indonesian defence zones, mostly by frontal infantry assaults with artillery and close air support. The Marine Bde made amphibious landings in East Java. The advances were hampered by many improvised mines, sabotage of roads and bridges, and roadblocks. Engagements were mostly sporadic; organized resistance was encountered

On 31 July 1947, immediately following the assault phase of Op 'Product', an 'OVW-er' Bren gunner from I-12 RI of X Bde provides cover during house searches in Malang, East Java. Section firepower was sometimes increased by the issue of a second Bren gun. See Plate E3 for uniform. (KTOMM Bronbeek, 2008/01/17-1-1/68)

at only a few points, in some cases broken by air support, and occasional Indonesian counterattacks were repulsed. Most *TNI* units and irregular groups evaded into difficult terrain and fled, thwarting the planned containment and destruction. The cost was that Dutch fatalities in the third quarter of 1947 rose sharply to *c.* 560. However, Op 'Product' was an operational success, dividing and reducing Republican territory and seriously disrupting *TNI* capabilities and plans.

General Spoor concluded on 24 July that the Republican government in Yogyakarta was unwilling or unable to comply with the Linggarjati treaty provisions, and argued for an expansion of his operation in order to occupy Yogyakarta. Van Mook was convinced, but the Dutch home government was not. The still-young United Nations Security Council intervened in the conflict on 1 August with Resolution 27, calling for a ceasefire and peace negotiations. These would be overseen by a Commission of Good Offices on the Indonesian Question (GOC) with military observers. The conflict had thus become internationalized.

TNI evacuations

Under the auspices of the UN, the Netherlands and the Republic of Indonesia concluded a ceasefire agreement on 17 January 1948 aboard the USS *Renville*, agreeing a truce along the so-called 'Van Mook' demarcation lines. Each side's troops would be evacuated into their own territory. Demilitarized zones were to be established between them, delineated by Dutch and Indonesian posts, with authority inside the DMZs exercised by civil police or military personnel under civil control. Politically, the Renville Agreement basically endorsed the Linggarjati draft.

Operation 'Product' had cut off an estimated 30,000 Republican troops and 120,000 non-state irregulars from unoccupied Republican territory, and about 29,000 *TNI* soldiers were evacuated from Dutch-occupied territory into Central Java. The Indonesian military was thus forced to abandon any hope of escalating the conflict in the medium term, and had to revert to defensive asymmetric warfare.

Pacification, 1947–48

Thereafter, the aims of the Dutch were the destruction of remaining Indonesian units; the restoration and maintenance of authority; and the security of important tactical, industrial and economic locations. This could only be achieved by dispersing the troops among the populations to be controlled, and by active and aggressive intelligence-led patrolling. The enemy had to be sought out and destroyed, and denied any opportunity to rest. Despite the ostensible 'truce', in the second half of 1948 Dutch fatalities rose again, from *c.* 200 to *c.* 800 per quarter.

The dispersed Dutch posts had defensive combat positions, and a field of fire about 300 metres deep. The perimeter was surrounded, at greater than grenade-throwing distance, with barbed wire obstacles fitted with noise-makers to warn of attempted infiltration, and mines and booby traps were also laid. Post garrisons were in company strength with at least two platoons, to defend the position while also sending out regular patrols. One-third of the patrols had to take place by night, to lay ambushes, while others might last several days. A number of post detachments would be placed under a sector commander, who coordinated the patrols with neighbouring sectors, and also formed a mobile reserve of at least one platoon with heavy infantry weapons. Intelligence personnel from the brigade HQ were attached to sector commands, and when concentrations of Indonesian troops were reported the Dutch mounted operations in anything up to brigade strength.

Operation 'Crow', 29 December 1948: airdrop by Para 1 company near Kenali Asam, South Sumatra, to capture the airfield and oilfield south of Jambi. During the whole operation the two companies of the Para Combat Group carried out three successive parachute assaults: on 19 and 29 December, and by the Para Co KST on 5 January 1949. (NIMH, 2155_023628)

Operation 'Crow', 1948–49

Despite Dutch efforts, the guerrillas grew in strength and insecurity increased, while political negotiations about the putative Dutch–Indonesian Union stalled. The Republic refused to dissolve its armed forces and to recognize the KNIL as the core of a new federal army under a temporary Dutch commander. Meanwhile, the Netherlands had to demobilize many troops whose term of service could not be extended any further. The financial costs were weighing heavily on the Dutch economy, and the beginning of the Cold War in Europe demanded attention.

Van Mook himself had now been succeeded by Crown High Commissioner, Louis Beel, who was persuaded by the military to support a second offensive to eliminate the Republican capital, Yogyakarta, as a centre of resistance. The Netherlands government gave in to persuasion at the end of 1948, even though the monsoon season was unfavourable for any rapid advances and for air support. The military goal of Operation 'Crow' (Kraai) was simply to eliminate both the Republic as a political entity and the *TNI*, again by applying the 'spearhead' doctrine. The objectives of its operational phases were:
• Occupation of Republican government centres at Yogyakarta, and Bukittingi (Fort de Kock) on Sumatra.
• Occupation of the other major cities and lines of communication.
• Encirclement and elimination of important enemy troop concentrations.

The Indonesians had anticipated a Dutch offensive against their Javanese capital. The *TNI* assumed that they would be unable to stop it, but could slow it down by 'scorched earth' tactics. Individual battalions would then withdraw into the countryside, before mounting infiltrations into Dutch-occupied territory. The Republican government planned to take refuge in friendly India until continued guerrilla warfare eventually forced the Dutch back to the negotiating table.

On 19 December 1948 a Combat Group M launched the offensive with a parachute drop by the Para Combat Group to capture Maguwo airfield near Yogyakarta. Subsequently, the Group's second echelon (rest

Operational area Tapanuli, North Sumatra, 1949. Following the occupation of the port of Sibolga ('12', centre left in bay) during Op 'Crow', the pacification phase saw many small posts established along the inland roads vulnerable to areas where TNI mobile forces were active (shaded here). Convoys were frequently attacked, and the necessary proliferation of posts (red dots) emphasizes the continuing strain on Dutch manpower in 1949. (KTOMM Bronbeek, 2019/08/28)

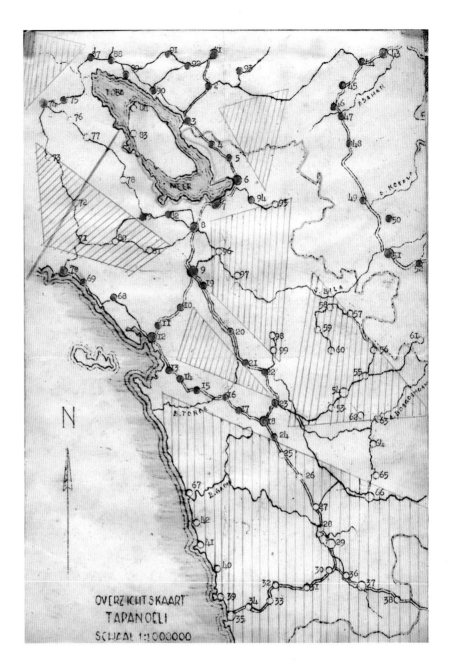

OVERZICHTSKAART
TAPANOELI
SCHAAL 1:1000000

of the KST, I-15 RI and 5-RS) was flown in to join them. Combat Group M occupied Yogyakarta the same day, capturing Soekarno, Hatta, and many other Indonesian government and military leaders. The third echelon follow-on force reached the capital overland from Semarang on 21 December.

B Division achieved most of its objectives in Central Java; *TNI* resistance was uneven but occasionally fierce, until broken by artillery fire and air support. However, the encirclement of the Div *Siliwangi* around Magelang failed, and it managed to escape westwards. The occupation and containment actions by A Div in East Java were seriously delayed by bridge and road sabotage. During an amphibious landing by the Marbrig at Glondong, a day's delay robbed them of tactical surprise. This allowed the Indonesians to put into effect their 'scorched earth' tactics, and the planned quick occupation of Cepu and Madiun failed. The 1st Inf Bde Group of C Div '7 December' occupied the Bantam area of south-west Java with little opposition.

On Sumatra, the Republican capital Bukittinggi was taken on 22 December. The Dutch carried out a combined airborne and amphibious operation near Jambi on 30 December: the Para Combat Group jumped south of Jambi, and two infantry companies were then flown in, while two more advanced by water. The oilfields and the town were occupied after fierce fighting, which partially destroyed both. The paratroopers jumped for the third time on 5 January 1949 at Rengat and Air Molek, occupying the oilfields.

In 1949, under the chairmanship of the United Nations Commission on Indonesia, military observers (MILOBs), Dutch and Indonesian officers met to discuss the boundaries of patrol areas and the subsequent transfer of territory. Here, on 21 October at Purworejo, Central Java, the Local Joint Committee 9 meets, its members wearing a left-arm 'LJC' brassard. From June 1949 the MILOBs (here, an Australian and a Belgian officer) wore a white brassard lettered 'KTN' (*Komisi Tiga Negara,* 'Three-State Commission') and 'UN' in dark blue. (National Archives, CC0; NL-HaNA_2.24.04.02_0_0831)

Guerrilla warfare, 1948–49

During and in the immediate aftermath of Op 'Crow' Indonesian troops initially clustered around the occupied towns and posts and launched guerrilla attacks, but soon afterwards they withdrew into their 'Wehrkreise'. Dutch (now, officially, 'Federal') territory was infiltrated, with the guerrillas focusing on the lines of communication, and soft targets such as collaborators, police, and agricultural estates; terror was employed to undermine government and economic reconstruction. Between 19 December 1948 and 31 July 1949 (according to probably incomplete Dutch figures) 943 Indonesian government officials and village chiefs were kidnapped and 560 murdered, with Central and East Java recording the most victims. The ever-present threat of such reprisals made cooperation with the Dutch increasingly unattractive to Indonesians.

On 22 December 1948 Col Nasution formally established a military administration over Java. The *TNI* was now fighting not only the Dutch, but also against communist and Islamic armed groups. (At a local level, this internal struggle sometimes even led to limited cooperation between the Dutch and Republicans.) The *TNI* managed to hold its own in large parts of Java and Sumatra, being especially active in recently-lost territory, but the surroundings of Jakarta, Semarang and Surabaya on Java, and Palembang, Medan and Padang on Sumatra remained firmly in Dutch hands.

Despite a reported deterioration in Dutch intelligence-gathering, on the tactical level the Dutch troops remained far superior. On 1 March 1949 a *TNI* brigade attacked Dutch-held Yogyakarta in what the nationalists called *Serangan Oemum 1 Maret 1949* ('General Attack 1 March

1949'), which was primarily intended to demonstrate to an international audience that the *TNI* was undefeated. It penetrated the city, but was driven out after the garrison received reinforcements; another attack on Surakarta, on 7 August, was also repulsed after four days. Following Op 'Crow', Dutch fatalities per quarter decreased from a peak of *c.*800 to *c.* 200 at the end of 1949, and during that whole year they claimed 47,000 Indonesians killed – a ratio of about 1: 24. On the other hand, the Dutch were now unable to make up their losses; their combat strength was slowly seeping away, while political developments had a negative impact on morale. According to Gen Spoor, by March 1949 the military struggle was only being waged in two isolated areas on Java and Sumatra, and beyond those only 'a completely unhinged armed youth' were operating. Nevertheless, at the end of March he spoke of an 18-month extension of the initially envisaged three to six months of pacification, and there would be no scope for troop reductions until after 1950. United Nations military observers reported that 'It is very apparent... that there are insufficient Dutch troops to control the area and ensure law and order; roving bands are moving freely and performing acts of sabotage daily...'.

The end, 1949–50
While doubts had taken root as early as March 1948, in the first quarter of 1949 the Dutch government rapidly lost confidence in a favourable military outcome. The Netherlands was no longer able to maintain a KL force of around 75,000 troops in the Indies, since rising tensions between NATO and the Soviet Union forced the government to focus its military attention in Europe. UN Security Council Resolution 63 of 24 December 1948 had instructed the warring parties to immediately cease hostilities and to release President Soerkarno and other political prisoners. Resolution 69 of 28 January 1949 repeated these demands, and instructed the Netherlands to transfer sovereignty to the United States of Indonesia by 1 July 1950 at the latest. The international community had turned against the Dutch recolonization policy, and the USA threatened to exclude the Netherlands from Marshall Aid and military support in Europe.

Finding itself politically isolated, and in a militarily hopeless dead-end, the Dutch government gave in. Their opponent Col Nasution would concede that 'The reason that the Dutch were finally willing to withdraw their forces... was not because they were defeated by our army, but because... there was no longer any hope for them to destroy the Republic.'

By the Van Roijen–Roem Declaration of 7 May 1949, the Netherlands recognized the Republic on Java and Sumatra as a sovereign entity within a United States of Indonesia, and the Republic undertook to cease guerrilla warfare. A Round Table Conference in The Hague would prepare for the transfer of sovereignty. On 3 August a ceasefire was agreed, which took effect on 11 August on Java and 15 August on Sumatra. On 27 December 1949 the Netherlands transferred sovereignty to the United States of Indonesia, still envisaging the formation of the Dutch–Indonesian Union. However, their Indonesian 'Federalist' collocutors were changing their minds: successively, the federal states merged, and the Republic of Indonesia became a unitary state on 17 August 1950. The Dutch–Indonesian Union remained a dead letter, and was unilaterally abandoned by Indonesia in 1956.

FURTHER READING

Anderson, Benedict R. O'G., *Java in a Time of Revolution, Occupation and Resistance 1944–1946* (Cornell University Press, 1972)

Bing Siong, H., 'The Secret of Major Kido. The Battle of Semarang, 15–19 October 1945', in *Bijdragen tot de Taal-, Land- en Volkenkunde 152 (1996) 3*, (Leiden), 382–428

Bing Siong, H., 'The Indonesian need of arms after the proclamation of independence', in *Bijdragen tot de Taal-, Land- en Volkenkunde 157 (2001) 4* (Leiden), 799–830

Bing Siong, H., 'Captain Huyser and the massive Japanese arms transfer in East Java in October 1945', in *Bijdragen tot de Taal-, Land- en Volkenkunde 159 (2003) 2/3* (Leiden), 291–350

Brocades Zaalberg, Thijs, 'The Civil and Military Dimensions of Dutch Counter–Insurgency on Java, 1947–1949', in *British Journal for Military History* (2015), 67–83

Connor, Stephen B., *Mountbatten's Samurai. Imperial Japanese Forces under British Control, 1945–1948* (Seventh Citadel, 2015)

Dijk, C. van, *Rebellion under the banner of Islam. The Darul Islam in Indonesia* (Verhandelingen van het Koninklijk Instituut voor Taal-, Land- en Volkenkunde, Martinus Nijhoff; The Hague, 1981)

Doorn, J.A.A. van & W.J. Hendrix, *Ontsporing van geweld. Over het Nederlands/Indisch/Indonesisch conflict* (Universitaire Pers Rotterdam, 1970)

Groen, P.M.H., *Marsroutes en dwaalsporen. Het Nederlands militair-strategisch beleid in Indonesië 1945–1950* (SDU Uitgeverij 's-Gravenhage, 1991)

Groen, Petra et al (eds), *Krijgsgeweld en kolonie. Opkomst en ondergang van Nederland als koloniale mogendheid 1816–2010* (Boom; Amsterdam, 2021)

Ham, M.L. van, 'Het Afwikkelingscommando van de Koninklijke Landmacht in Indonesië (1950–1951)', in *Mars et Historia. Orgaan van de Nederlandse Vereniging ter beoefening van de militaire historie* (1974): 8–5, 12–16; 8–6, 26–28; 9–1, 4–6 & 9: (1975) 3–5–10

Hoed, A. den, 'Het KNIL in de knel. De ontbinding van het KNIL en het lot van de militairen', in Teitler G. & J. Hoffenaar (eds), *De Politionele Acties. Afwikkeling en verwerking* (De Bataafsche Leeuw; Amsterdam, 1990), 21–33

Hoekstra, Martin, *De Republiek in een wurggreep. De Nederlandse marineblokkade tijdens de Indonesische Onafhankelijkheidsoorlog (1945–1949)*, masterscriptie Faculteit der Geesteswetenschappen (Universiteit Leiden, 2018)

Holst Pellekaan, R.E. van & I.C. de Regt, *Operaties in de oost. De Koninklijke Marine in de Indische archipel 1945–1951* (De Bataafsche Leeuw, 2003)

IJzereef, Willem, *De Zuid-Celebes Affaire. Kapitein Westerling en de standrechtelijke executies* (De Bataafsche Leeuw; Dieren, 1984)

Limpach, Rémy, *De brandende kampongs van Generaal Spoor* (Boom; Amsterdam, 2016), 142 Margadant, L., 'De Politie-organisatie in het nieuwe Bestel', in *Bestuursvraagstukken. Soal-soal pemerintahan, 1* (1949, 2), 190–197

Margadant, L., 'Ondernemingswachten', in *Bestuursvraagstukken. Soal-soal pemerintahan, 1* (1949, 3), 325–333

McMillan, Richard, *The British Occupation of Indonesia 1945–1946. Britain, the Netherlands and the Indonesian revolution* (Routledge; London, New York & Amsterdam, 2005)

Nasution, A.H., *Fundamentals of Guerrilla Warfare*, 2nd edn (Seruling Masa; Djakarta, 1970) Oosteinde, Gert, Ben Schoenmaker & Frank van Vree (eds), *Beyond the Pale. Dutch extreme violence in the Indonesian War of Independence, 1945–1949* (Amsterdam University Press, 2022)

Remmelink, W.G.J., 'The emergence of a new situation: the Japanese army on Java after the surrender' in *Militaire Spectator* (1987), 49–66

Schoonoord, D.C.L., *De Mariniersbrigade 1943–1949. Wording en inzet in Indonesië* (Afdeling Maritieme Historie van de Marinestaf; 's-Gravenhage, 1988)

Vogelpoel, J.F.R. van, *De Koninklijke Landmacht na de Tweede Wereldoorlog. Hoofddeel II. De opbouw ten behoeve van de pacificatie van Nederlands-Indië 5 mei 1945–27 december 1949* (Krijgsgeschiedkundige Afdeling – HKG; 's-Gravenhage, 1959)

Ward, O.G., *De Militaire Luchtvaart van het KNIL in de na-oorlogse jaren 1945–1950* (Unieboek Houten, 1988)

Winter, Th. de, 'Het Kon. Nederl. Indonesische Leger. Het leger in Indonesië', in *Militaire Spectator* (1948), 267–281

Zijlmans, G.C., *Eindstrijd en ondergang van de Indische Bestuursdienst. Het corps binnenlands bestuur op Java 1945–1950* (De Bataafsche Leeuw, 1985)

Zwitser, H.L. (ed), *Documenten betreffende de Eerste Politionele Actie (20/21 juli–4 augustus 1947)* (Sectie Militaire Geschiedenis van de Landmachtstaf; 's-Gravenhage, 1983)

PLATE COMMENTARIES

A: THE *BERSIAP*, 1945
A1: *Pemuda*
A rank-and-file revolutionary was called a *pemuda* or *pemudi* (Indonesian for 'young man' and 'young woman'). They had often received rudimentary training in youth organizations during the Japanese occupation, though normally only with bamboo spears *(bambu runcing)*. These traditional weapons, often with the point hardened by fire, together with *golok* machetes, were widely used during the killings of later 1945. Wearing uniforms was generally seen as 'non-revolutionary'; a *pemuda* should look like a rebel, growing his hair long, and dressed and armed with whatever he could lay his hands on. The basic Republican insignia is the *merah putih* (red/white) patch pinned to his vest.

A2: *Pemudi, Barisan Pemberontakan Rajkat Indonesia*
Women nationalists took an active part in the armed struggle; often students, they formed their own political organizations or separate women's sections. This 'Indonesian People's Revolutionary Front', formed in October 1945 and active around Surabaya, Malang and Yogyakarta, was described as the most revolutionary group of all. The girl wears men's clothing with a 'B.P.R.I.' brassard taped around her left arm.

A nationalist *pemuda* machine-gunner (left) with his assistant; the partly visible weapon may be a 7.7mm Japanese Type 97 aircraft gun modified for ground use. The rebel fighters appear to be dressed in white, as was common, and wear straw hats. The youth on the left is growing his hair long – many had vowed not to cut their hair until Indonesia became independent. (IPPHOS, 0063)

The pre-war KNIL 6.5mm Mannlicher M95 carbine, retrieved from Japanese arsenals, was a common weapon among non-state armed groups.

A3: *Pemuda, Tentara Peladjar*
This member of the 'Students Army' *(TP)*, which was later absorbed into the *TNI*, is dressed in black, apart from a Japanese helmet painted with a Republican red/white disc. He has armed himself with a Japanese Nambu 8mm Type 14 semi-automatic pistol, and a Japanese *shin-gunto* military sword, probably made locally during the occupation.

B: REPUBLICAN POLICE & ARMY, 1946–49
B1: *Komisaris kl I,* Republican police, 1948
After the August 1945 capitulation this force remained responsible for law and order; it retained its small arms and also, significantly, several dozen light and heavy machine guns. After entering Republican service in September/October 1945 the police prioritized the independence struggle over law enforcement. Many young men enlisted in regular and auxiliary branches, and a paramilitary *Barisan Polisi Istimewa* ('Special Police Legion') was formed. This officer displays the cap badge of the Republican police. His rank of assistant superintendent is identified by two gold stars on his shoulder straps, and three gold stripes and a button on his black collar patches.

B2: *Sersan kl II, Tentara Republik Indonesia,* 1946–47
The armed forces of the Republic showed a diverse variety of clothing; while some had uniforms, others, as here, wore combinations of civilian and military garments. The *TRI* black sidecap (note flap cut like a US 'garrison cap') bears a Republican oval metal badge divided diagonally red over white. The Japanese-style rank patch of sergeant 2nd class – a sky-blue rhomboid bearing a silver star on a gold stripe – is pinned to his left chest. He is armed with a British 9mm Sten sub-machine gun, but for lack of equipment has to carry the spare magazine in his trouser pocket.

B3: *Major, Tentara National Indonesia,* 1949
After the ceasefire in 1949 the *TNI* was supplied with uniforms via the Dutch army, and this major wears Dutch jungle-green battledress with its distinctive pockets on the front of both thighs. The gold badge on his cap bears a metal star above the wreathed 'RI' monogram *(Republik Indonesia)*. Alternatively, berets or peaked caps might be worn with the same badge. Just visible on the shirt collar points are silver 'TNI' monograms. Early in 1949 the army changed the previously Japanese-type officers' rank insignia, of rectangular patches on the collar or left chest, to a black square on shoulder-strap slip-ons. Here the major's gold star is set on a gold-bordered black square, 'below' the brass crossed rifles of the infantry. (Under this system NCOs and enlisted ranks wore chevrons and stripes respectively, on upper-sleeve patches.) He wears a mixture of British and US belt-order webbing, with a holstered Colt M1911 .45 ACP semi-automatic pistol.

B4: *TRI* divisional flag, 1948
Divisional flags were presented on 5 October 1946. This example was captured at Surakarta, Central Java, in December 1948. We have been unable to reconcile it with the known order of battle, but it bears the lettering *TENTARA/R.I./ANGKATAN DARAT/DIVISIE/GUNA WARMAN*.

C: REPUBLICAN NAVY & AIR FORCE
C1: *Pradjurit II, Angkatan Laut Republik Indonesia,* 1946
The Republican Navy *(ALRI)* was dressed in white or khaki uniform with trousers or shorts and a white cap. This seaman 2nd class wears a blue-edged white 'jumper' modelled on that of the Imperial Japanese Navy, with a matching undershirt and sailor collar. The cap ribbon was lettered 'A.L.R.I.', with or without a central anchor badge. Ratings displayed rank insignia on a removable black tin shield on the left sleeve: for petty officers, painted gold chevrons beneath a gold fouled anchor, and for seamen these red bars above a red anchor.

C2: Tjalon Letnan, ALRI
Officers and warrant officers wore either white or khaki working dress of a short-sleeved military shirt and shorts, and a white cap resembling the Italian 'bustina' rather than the usual sidecap. The photo which we copy here shows an officer wearing the white shirt under the khaki one, with its collar folded outside. Officers' rank was displayed on black removable shoulder boards – here the single gold stripe with a 'curl' of a sub-lieutenant.

C3: Kadet Udara I, Angkatan Udara Republik Indonesia
The badge of the Republican Air Force (AURI) was the garuda, a part-human, part-eagle mythical creature. This flight lieutenant's headgear is a British RAF-blue sidecap with two gold frontal buttons, and a gold garuda on the front right. Rank is shown by two short gold stripes and a garuda on full-length black slip-ons on his shoulder straps. The more junior officer ranks (ensign, second lieutenant, and cadet) wore silver insignia, and the garuda was in gold, silver or brass depending upon rank class. Sersan and kopral displayed a brass garuda above white chevrons on a black patch on the upper left sleeve, where privates wore the garuda and one or two white stripes.

C4: Alternative ALRI officers' ranking
On ALRI working uniform officers might display their rank on tin rhomboids on both collars; here, the gold stripes identify a kapten (lieutenant-commander).

D: ROYAL NETHERLANDS–INDIES FORCES, 1946–49
D1: Ambonese infantryman, KNIL
Ambonese soldiers were thought to have better military qualities than other Indonesians, by a Dutch variant of the 'martial races' theory. In 1946 it was recommended that KNIL troops on Java be temporarily supplied with American field dress, while those in the Outer Regions could use the Australian type which was the preferred choice for the long term. This Ambonese infantry private (Soldaat) wears the Australian 1943 jungle-green cotton half-buttoning shirt, and trousers varying from the British type in lacking the left-thigh frontal pocket. (While individual garments naturally varied in shade with age and laundering, the issue trousers did come in a greyer shade than the shirt.) His headgear is an Indian-made British jungle-green cotton GS (general service) cap, and his boots are KNIL black canvas and leather field shoes worn with British woollen ankle puttees. His web equipment is an Australian variant of British Ptn 37 with extra-broad reinforcement to the shoulder braces, and his weapon is a .303in Lee Enfield Mk V 'jungle carbine'.

D2: Korporaal, VK-KNIL
The Women's Corps of the KNIL was temporarily established in Australia in March 1944, and permanently incorporated in February 1946. The first volunteers came from Australia and Surinam, but later from Canada, the USA and the Netherlands. Applicants had to be Dutch nationals 18–45 years old and having a high-school diploma; only a small number were locally recruited in the Indies as parachute-packers. At its peak the VK-KNIL numbered 519 women, mostly performing clerical, hospital and welfare duties throughout the archipelago. This corporal wears khaki cotton shirtsleeve working dress; a four-pocket bush jacket with integral cloth belt was also available. The headgear, again cut like a US 'garrison cap', bears at front left the brass national badge of a crowned lion rampant on a scroll. Slip-ons on the shoulder straps display her rank insignia on a universal black triangle backing, below the Medical Corps badge of her assignment (see 2a). At the top of the sleeves is pinned a voided brass title, 'V.K. K.N.I.L.' between horizontal lines.

D3: Onderluitenant pilot, ML-KNIL
Men of this KNIL rank, equivalent to chief warrant officer, performed officers' duties. The black-banded, khaki-crowned service dress peaked cap bears the elaborate gold metal and embroidered ML-KNIL officer's badge. After landing his B-25 Mitchell, he has put the cap on in place of his US AN-10A flying helmet. His OD gabardine flying overalls are the USAAF Type

A-4, here a variant with shoulder straps, with khaki slip-ons displaying the two silver half-balls of his rank on the KNIL black triangle. On his left chest he has added privately-purchased brass pilot/observer's 'wings', and his shoulder holster holds a Colt M1911 pistol.

E: NETHERLANDS ROYAL ARMY, 1947–48
E1: Soldaat 1ste klasse, 7 Regiment Infanterie
This lance-corporal equivalent wears combat gear for a short-range patrol. Copied in the Netherlands from British models, his jungle-green bush jacket is worn tucked into battledress trousers with the distinctive Dutch paired frontal thigh pockets (though British issue was also seen). Instead of an American or British steel helmet he wears a US Army herringbone-twill (HBT) field cap in Olive Drab Shade 7; his boots are KNIL black canvas and leather field shoes, and his web anklets are British surplus. On the shoulder-strap slip-ons are his white rank chevron and the yellow-on-blue regimental title '7 R.I.'. The use of chevrons on shoulder straps instead of on the sleeve was prohibited until introduced by Army Order No. 57 of 9 November 1946. Pausing for a drink from his British canteen (taken from its carrier buckled below the back of his belt), he has slung his Canadian-made .303in Lee Enfield No. 4 Mk I* rifle. His webbing is British Ptn 37, but with two pairs of 'cartridge carriers' instead of two large 'basic pouches'; since the former held only 40 rounds, he has a five-pocket, 50-round cotton bandolier slung around his waist, with its tape tucked above the spike bayonet frogged on the left of his belt. He probably also has a magazine for the section's Bren gun in each leg pocket, and a No.36 fragmentation grenade in his left chest pocket; note the round for the platoon's 2in mortar crammed into the other.

Detail from a photo of Republican police officers parading at Bangil, near Pasuruan in East Java during 1947. Compare uniforms with Plate B1, and note the klewang cutlasses. (NIMH, 2174–1733)

E2: Majoor, Regiment Huzaren van Boreel, walking-out dress

The khaki cotton walking-out dress, with shorts or long trousers, was basically the same for all branches, but Army Order No.57 introduced distinctive unit insignia. This commander of an armoured car squadron has the cavalry's black beret, with a silver regimental badge of St George and the Dragon on a bright blue backing edged with dark blue. Shoulder-strap slip-ons display the silver cavalry branch badge 'above' his ranking of a silver bar and gold star. The dark khaki 'rocker'-shaped national insignia at the top of his left sleeve bears in orange-yellow the Dutch rampant lion emblem above a new 1947 scroll, 'JE MAINTIENDRAI'. Below this is the patch (see **2a**) common to the 1st to 3rd Armoured Car Squadrons. Invisible on his upper right sleeve is the crowned 'OVW' patch of a war volunteer (see **2b**). All these badges, removable for the laundering of clothes, might be either embroidered on cloth or painted on metal.

E3: Infantry Bren-gunner

The infantry platoon establishment was 37 all ranks, comprising a 7-man platoon HQ including a 2in mortar detachment, and three 10-man sections (squads). The section had a 7-man rifle group led by the sergeant, and a 3-man Bren group led by

Miss Josephine Willinck was born in October 1925 in Kertosono, East Java. During World War II she lived in France, and from September 1943 she was involved in the Resistance. From November 1944 to April 1945 she worked for the Americans in Paris as a tri-lingual interpreter, telephone operator and driver. She joined the VK-KNIL in London on 25 June 1945, and was sent to Australia as a driver, later being promoted to sergeant. For uniform, compare with Plate D2. (National Archives, CC0; NL-HaNA_2.24.04.03_0_10665)

the corporal second-in-command. Officially, platoon firepower was one revolver, 4 Sten SMGs, 29 rifles, 3 Bren guns, a 2in mortar, and 36 hand grenades. This Bren 'No.1' carries the Mk 3 gun, with a shortened barrel for use by paratroops and in the Far East. His British Mk II helmet has a string net and hessian 'scrim' for camouflage. The 1942 US Army one-piece camouflage overall had usefully large expanding pockets, but was notoriously unpopular with World War II 'GIs' for its weight, heat, and sanitary inconvenience; nevertheless, it was widely used in the Netherlands Indies. The web equipment is British Ptn 37, with the 'basic' pouches that each held two Bren magazines.

F: NETHERLANDS ROYAL NAVY, KNIL PARATROOPS & SPECIAL FORCES
F1: Sergeant, KM, 1945

On 16 September 1945 the KM cruiser HNLMS *Tromp* entered the harbour of Batavia (Jakarta) at Tanjung Priok. At the end of the month the *Tromp* contributed a naval landing division of four officers and 100 seamen to operate against *pemudas* in Jakarta. In the tropics the KM wore khaki working dress or white daily dress. Ratings wore their white 'jumper' (borstrok) with khaki shorts, and white-covered sailor caps with yellow lettering 'KONINKLYKE (or 'KONINKLIJKE) MARINE' on the black ribbon 'tally'. Petty officers wore military shirts and a peaked cap. Commanding a checkpoint, this petty officer 1st class of the landing division displays his ranking – a black square with gold braid edging at front and bottom – on his shirt collar. He wears Australian jungle-green trousers, with British woollen ankle puttees and black boots. He is armed with an M95 carbine and a KNIL cutlass (klewang) hanging from its looped wrist strap, and has an obsolete rifle cartridge box on his belt.

F2: KNIL paratrooper, SOP, 1947

The 1941 reorganization of the KNIL had included the creation of an Experimental Parachutist Unit (Proefafdeling Parachutisten); at least eight soldiers were trained, but no operational unit was formed. In 1946 the KNIL picked up the thread again with a Paratroop Training School (SOP), which later formed an operational company. This Indonesian paratrooper is instructing with the Australian 9mm Owen Mk I/43 'machine carbine', which was superior to both the Thompson and the Sten. He wears the maroon beret introduced in mid-1947, badged with a brass winged wreath showing a parachute above a fist-and-dagger. His one-piece overall is locally made from camouflage material based on the US 1942 pattern; it also differs in having shoulder straps, and pockets low outside the legs, and is worn with US web leggings and russet field shoes.

F2a: Painted metal SOP left-sleeve badge
F3: KNIL commando, DST, 1948

The KNIL Special Forces Depot (DST), established in 1946, followed the traditions of both the British World War II commandos (of which some Dutch veterans served as instructors), and the pre-war elite counter-guerrilla Korps Marechaussee in Aceh, Sumatra. In addition to a parachute-trained company, in 1948 it formed two rifle companies designated Troops II and III. In Op 'Crow' the Para Co KST made a combat jump, while these companies carried out an air-landing operation on Java, and then fought in the ground offensive in Central Sumatra. In 1946 the KNIL in Java were issued US OD two-piece HBT field uniforms of the late 1942 pattern with large cargo pockets. Only slightly contrasting in this painting, the headgear is in fact the British commando-green wool beret; the brass Dutch lion badge worn on a square black backing has a scroll lettered 'NED. INDIE'. With his HBT shirt and trousers, this Indonesian or Eurasian commando wears US canvas-and-rubber jungle boots; he is armed with a Thompson SMG, and carries the *klewang* as a jungle machete slung from a US M1923 rifle belt.

F3a: Painted metal DST left-sleeve badge

G: KM MARBRIG & MARVA

G1: BAR gunner, Marine infantry
The Mariniersbrigade, equipped in the USA in 1944–45, was issued with USMC field uniform. The marine platoon establishment was one officer and 45 NCOs and enlisted men, organized in a 6-man HQ and three rifle squads.The heavily-armed 13-man rifle squad consisted of a sergeant squad leader, and three automatic rifle teams of 4 men each: a corporal team leader, an automatic rifleman with the .30cal M1918A2 BAR, his assistant, and one other rifleman. In the USMC 1944 platoon the officer, squad leaders and assistant BAR gunners were issued M1 carbines.This marine wears the M1 helmet with USMC second-pattern HBT reversible camouflage cover; the USMC P1941 sage-green HBT 'utilities', with the shirt tucked into the trousers, which are bloused over web leggings, and russet field shoes. The USMC left-chest stencil is hidden in this pose; the Dutch marines also followed USMC style in hand-painting rank insignia on field uniform – for officers and warrant officers, in yellow on the collar, and for NCOs in black on the upper left sleeve. The visible web equipment is the M1937 six-pouch BAR belt with suspenders and first aid pouch, with one or perhaps two canteens hooked to the back of the belt.

G2: Marine tank crewman
The Marbrig's TANKCO was established on 22 April 1946, with 179 all ranks in a company HQ and three platoons, totalling 17 M4A3 Sherman tanks and one recovery tank. With the later downsizing of the brigade, the company was disbanded in December 1947. This member of a five-man Sherman crew wears the P1944 second pattern of the sage-green HBT utilities, again with the jacket tucked in. In the Marbrig the 'USMC' and eagle, globe and anchor stencil on the single left chest pocket were sometimes retained, sometimes scrubbed off as far as was possible. The fibre tank helmet is the M1941 with R14 headphones, and N-2 goggles. He is armed with an M1911 Colt pistol in a shoulder holster, and carries on his pistol belt its two-magazine pouch and a 'Ka bar' knife.

G3: MARVA 1ste klasse
In 1944 a Netherlands women's naval service (MARVA) was established, and by 1 January 1949 some 191 women were serving at Jakarta and Surabaya. The tropical daily uniform for ratings consisted of a white sailor cap with the black ribbon lettered 'KONINKLIJKE MARINE' in yellow; a short-sleeved white blouse; a long skirt fastened with three buttons on the left; a whitened canvas 'money belt'; and either white or black shoes. Ratings wore chevrons on a removable navy-blue backing on the left sleeve – red below the rank of Chief MARVA, and light blue above.

H: CIVIL SERVICE, GENERAL POLICE, & PAT

H1: Controleur 1ste klasse, 1946–49
Under the British, the militarized Netherlands Indies Civil Administration (NICA) was briefly renamed Allied Military Administration Civil Affairs Branch (AMACAB). After the British departure, in November 1946 the name was changed to Temporary Administrative Service. This assistant district officer wears a khaki bush jacket with shorts, and a peaked cap with a khaki crown and a patterned black band. The gold-embroidered cap badge is a crowned wreath and Dutch national lion shield, and the crown is repeated above the two gold rank bars on his black shoulder-strap slip-ons. In view of the insecurity, this administrative officer is armed with a 1931 model .38cal Colt Police Positive revolver, in a leather civilian holster on an American web pistol belt.

H2: Commissaris, Algemene Politie, 1947
After the departure of British troops the Netherlands Indies police force was completely reorganized. This General Police had a unit in each territorial administrative 'residence', commanded by a Commissaris; in the newly formed federal states it was reorganized into state (negara) police. After Op 'Product' in 1947, local (daerah) police were also formed in newly-reoccupied territory. The General Police wore white or khaki service and green field uniforms. This Eurasian commissioner wears the white cap, bush jacket and trousers, with removable gilt buttons. The gilt cap badge is an elaborate crowned, wreathed national coat-of-arms, which is repeated in miniature above two six-point gold rank stars on the shoulder-strap slip-ons.

H3: Chinese volunteer, Pao An Tui, 1947
The Chinese-Indonesian community of about 1.2 million made up some 2 per cent of the total population. They were mainly economically active in commerce and industry on Java, as coolies on European agricultural estates in East Sumatra, or in tin-mining. The Indonesian revolutionaries were violently hostile to this ethnic group, and they suffered badly during the Bersiap and subsequent killings. By the end of 1945 the community had formed a self-defence force, the Pao An Tui (PAT), in places where there was a substantial Chinese presence. The Dutch assisted in training and supplied arms for static security duties, though patrolling was officially forbidden. The PAT was (partly) uniformed and badged, and its political association with the Kuomintang in China is reflected by the cap of this volunteer's khaki uniform. Note cap badge in (3a); the larger silver-on-black sleeve badge was rather more elaborate, incorporating Chinese characters and a chain-link border.

With the decision to disband the KNIL, its personnel faced either transfer into the Indonesian armed forces (APRIS) or the Dutch metropolitan forces, or demobilization. This sergeant of Inf I battalion transferred to the APRIS on 27 May 1950 at Bogor, with simultaneous promotion to lieutenant. On his right he still wears KNIL rank insignia, and on his left he places that of the APRIS. (IPPHOS, 1695)

INDEX

Note: locators in bold refer to plates, illustrations and captions.